American Rally Action 2

American Rally Action 2

Ronnie Arnold

SPEED-PICS Publishing

ISBN 10: 0-9778320-1-5
ISBN 13: 978-0-9778320-1-9

Library of Congress Control Number: 2006902504

Printed in China

Book design and production: Tabby House
Cover design: Juanita Dix
Cover background photos: Jupiter Images

SPEED-PICS Publishing
6101 Long Prairie Road, #744-110
Flower Mound, TX 75028
www.speed-pics.com

Contents

Appendices

Foreword

It is almost twenty years since an American driver, the young John Buffum, attained a podium finish on an FIA World Championship Rally, and it is something that we in the rally circus find is disappointing. But rally talent does not grow on trees, and especially in barren areas, and in some ways the dearth of American international rally talent does not come as a great surprise. To revert to former glories means we need a rebirth of interest in rallying as we know it in the United States. The current resurgence of interest in rallying in America therefore brings with it a lot of hope and excitement.

The sport does not breed its drivers by the efforts of the drivers alone. This comes from having a strong grassroots background, and that comes from the enthusiasm and expertise of everyone involved in the sport. Sébastien Loeb did not just happen to win the Monte Carlo Rally. Rally Norway did not just happen to enter the world championship. Ford did not just happen to design a rally winning Focus RS World Rally Car. Everything that succeeds in the sport does so as a result of hard work, determination and flair from everyone involved. I can see the way that this is happening in America right now.

In the years when the World Championship was less time-consuming as now, it was my pleasure to attend a lot of rallies in the United States. I think that something absolutely memorable happened on every trip I made from Europe. I met dedicated professionals, all of whom achieved good results whenever they went abroad, as well as passionate enthusiasts who gave the sport their every moment's attention. One of the ways that this spirit can truly return is by access to good information back home. There is no more effective way of registering and recording what happens than in what Ronnie Arnold is doing in his *Rally Action* book.

I wish Ronnie every success in this project, and heartily recommend his endeavours. This project is more than an appendage to the sport. It is the reason why the sport in America has the chance to progress into the future. And maybe, an American incarnation of John Buffum will be seen standing on the podium of a world championship rally again in the future!

Martin Holmes, publisher
Pirelli World Rallying annual books

Introduction

I was standing deep in a forest, feeling cold and wet. I was waiting for the first cars, but my mind was wandering and I started to think, "Why has no one done a book of rallying in the USA?" Something like Martin Holmes' *World Rallying* on a local scale.

I looked around furtively—as if some of the other photographers enjoying the freezing conditions would be able to read my mind—and decided it was worth exploring the idea further.

After a ten-month shooting season and a further six months of writing and editing, I met my first copies of *American Rally Action* at a motel in Wellsboro, Pennsylvania. They had been sent by air courier direct to STPR. The bulk of the books would arrive by ship several weeks later. My excitement was intense and I was pleased with the results, though having spent many hours with the galley proofs there were not many surprises. What was more important was the experience when I brought the books to the technical inspection and asked BerylAnn from Rally America to put them on her stand.

I watched from a distance as a potential customer approached, picked up a copy of the book and started to flick through it. His girlfriend was looking over his shoulder. I held my breath wondering whether he would like it or not. He stood there a long time, turning the pages, until I could not wait any longer—I had to go and take care of some other business. Some time later I returned and he was still there, turning the pages. Finally he put his hand in his pocket and took out the requisite cash to buy the copy. I had made my first sale at an event.

The feedback I have received about the first book has been amazing. And has been enough to persuade me to continue to produce this second volume. The fact that American rallying has continued to grow and strengthen has been an additional motivator. In 2006 we saw the return of manufacturer-supported teams with Vermont SportsCar entries in Subaru colors and we saw both championships adding events to their calendars.

That's not to say that everything in the American rallying "garden" is rosy. Having two championships in such a small market causes confusion for the competitors. The great distances that teams have to travel makes the cost of competing at the national level almost prohibitive. Yet the inherent spectacle of the sport and the adrenaline it generates for any driver, co-driver and engineer makes it addictive enough to keep the teams coming back.

In the 2006 Rally America championship, Travis Pastrana was a popular overall winner and has to be one of the best ambassadors the American rallying scene has had. In 2007 he is scheduled to compete in selected World Rally Championship events and I know everyone will be wishing him every success.

In the U.S. Rally Championship, Seamus Burke proved that a strong car and experienced driver can make a formidable team. His championship was well deserved.

I hope you enjoy this second volume of *American Rally Action*.

Acknowledgments

When I finally got done with putting together *American Rally Action*, I swore "never again." The hours of work—especially writing reports—just did not seem to justify the end result. Yet here I am publishing a second volume. My change of heart can be put squarely at the feet of all the enthusiasts who encouraged me throughout the year. The feedback I have received has been universally positive, and without that feedback I would not have considered a second volume. So to all my readers, "Thank you."

My efforts pale to insignificance compared to the work involved in organizing an event. Once again this year, my thanks to all the event teams from the Rally America and the U.S. Rally championships. Not only do they make the events happen, they have supported me when I visit their areas, helped me find the best photographic locations and even help me sell my books. I thank them for their permission to reproduce their logos and the event and championship results. Their copyright is hereby recognized.

Of course it is the competitors who make my efforts worthwhile and who create the photogenic opportunities. I have always made it my goal to get the best possible shots without putting myself, or the teams, at risk. My thanks to them for helping me; and my best wishes for a successful and safe season.

Early drafts of the book were checked for accuracy by Bruce Weinman and Beryl Ann Burton whose generous assistance I want to acknowledge.

I have made every effort to ensure accuracy throughout the book but, being human, I am sure that errors have crept in. All errors are mine and mine alone.

Once again this year I have depended heavily on the experienced assistance of Jim and Linda Salisbury of Tabby House. Last year taught me how much there is to publishing a book, enough to know I could not achieve it alone. Without their help this book would not happen.

Sno*Drift Rally
Lewiston, Michigan
January 27–28, 2006

*Above: Andrew Comrie-Picard / Rod Hendricksen win the 2006 Sno*Drift.*

Left: Andrew Pinker / Robbie Durant on the practice stage.

Sno*Drift Rally, the traditional first round of the Rally America season, followed its regular format using the snow-packed roads around Montmorency County over two days of competition.

The weather was unseasonably warm—with temperatures rising from an overnight low in the twenties to a peak in the mid-fifties. Fortunately, there was no snow—or rain—but still, the road surface was firm and icy.

Last year's winner and series champion, Pat Richard, had not entered but there was a good over-all entry with series regulars including Matt Iorio with Ole Holter co-driving, Otis Dimiters with Alan Ockwell and Tanner Foust with Scott Crouch. Andrew Comrie-Picard (ACP) had entered with co-driver Rod Hendricksen with overseas entries from Australian Andrew Pinker with Robbie Durant and Alfredo de Dominicis (Dedo) from Italy, co-driven by Mike Rossey.

The big change for the season, though, was the return of Subaru, which had provided works support to the Vermont SportsCar team of Travis Pastrana / Christian Edstrom and Ken Block /

Above: J. B. Niday (R) talks with Matt Iorio.

Stop sign for more than vehicles.

Alessandro Gelsomino. The event had forty-eight entries of which twenty-six were running at the national level.

As in previous years, the event started on Friday afternoon with the short, fast downhill run on the King-Scenic stage. Fastest time was posted by Iorio—covering the 1.6 miles in one minute, fifty-six seconds. Two seconds behind him came Block then ACP. But the news from the stage was about de Dominicis who retired having crashed heavily within a quarter mile of the start.

The second stage, Fish Lab, was another short one. Fastest time went to Pinker then Pastrana and Iorio. This was followed by two longer stages—The Ranch and Greasy Creek. Iorio showed his mettle on The Ranch taking it in eleven minutes and ten seconds—a full seventeen seconds ahead of second place Block then Pinker. On Greasy Creek it was Block followed by Pastrana then ACP. Iorio dropped a minute due to a flat tire.

Left: Karen Purzycki / Bob Pierce in their colorful Ford Fiesta.

Dimiters / Ockwell pulled off after stage 2 with a small fire that caused them to retire on the transit road.

So, as the teams rolled into first service, it was a one-two for the Subaru team with Block leading Pastrana by just under thirty seconds.

The first day would conclude with three night stages: Halberg, East Fish Lake and a repeat visit to The Ranch. Pastrana would take his first fastest time of the event on Halberg, followed by Pinker and Block. The stage would catch Iorio, who rolled about a mile into it and retired. On East Fish Lake it was Pinker's turn to claim fastest time with Pastrana and Block close behind—a sequence that was repeated on the last stage of the evening.

At the end of the first day, it was Pinker holding an eighteen-second lead over Block and Pastrana; although it was still anyone's event for the taking.

The weather held for Saturday. The teams were due to compete on ninety miles over ten stages including two runs on the almost twenty-five mile That Old Black River.

Throughout the day it was a close fight among five teams. Block took the first stage of the day from Pastrana, Pinker and ACP; then Pastrana took one on Camp 24-25. It was ACP who won on That Old Black River from Pinker then Foust, who had been picking up speed. Pinker lost twenty minutes when he went into a ditch and Pastrana had a double-flat when he hit a rock. He had to complete fourteen miles of stage before service—losing six minutes to the leaders and ending his chances of a good placing.

After lunch, Foust showed his control of the Production GT class Subaru by coming first on

Above and below: Pete Hascher / Scott Rhoades make full use of the snowbanks.

Travis Pastrana / Christian Edstrom clear the snow on their way to second overall.

John Buffum (L) talks with Ken Block.

Meaford, second on the second running of That Old Black River and another first on Hungry Five. He was swapping seconds with Block, Pastrana and Pinker. As the crews came in for the evening service, Foust had climbed to second overall behind ACP. Pastrana and Block were lying in third and fourth.

The evening session continued the close fight. Stage wins went to Pastrana, Block and Foust, with Pinker and ACP always close-by.

The event did not finish with the last stage, as a number of cars were found to be running with rule violations. After review, the stewards decided to let the results stand as-is but gave a number of competitors warnings for future events.

The final result and Open Class win went to Comrie-Picard / Hendricksen who, despite only having won one stage, showed that in the snow consistency is everything. Behind them, Pastrana / Edstrom came second and Foust / Crouch third, also taking the PGT class.

Greg Drozd / Chris Gordon light up the Gene Henderson Memorial stage.

Other class wins went to Pinker / Durant in Group N; Michael Merbach / Jeff Feldt in Production; Eric Burmeister / Dave Shindle in Group 5 and Eric Duncan / Matt Duncan in Group 2.

Sno*Drift Rally - Schedule

Stage #	First Car	Stage Name	Miles
Friday, January 27			
	14:31	Rally Start - Lewiston	
1	14:46	King Scenic	1.63
2	15:14	Fish Lab	2.68
3	15:50	The Ranch 1	7.34
4	16:27	Greasy Creek	8.28
		Service - Lewiston	
5	18:52	Halberg	2.72
6	19:16	East Fish Lake	8.61
7	19:58	The Ranch 2	7.34
Saturday, January 28			
8	9:13	Jackpine Trail	2.33
9	9:45	Camp 24-25	7.60
10	10:34	That Old Black River 1	24.68
		Service - Atlanta	
11	13:17	Meaford	7.74
12	13:59	That Old Black River 2	24.68
13	14:41	Hungry Five - 1	3.46
		Service - Atlanta	
14	17:12	Gene Henderson Memorial	5.05
15	17:44	DeCheau-Mills	4.72
16	18:12	Hungry Five - 2	3.46
17	18:51	Thunder River	5.94
	19:21	Rally Finish - Hillman	

Henry Krolikowski / Cindy Krolikowski drove their Subaru to fifth overall.

Mark McElduff / Damian Irwin did not see out the first day.

Norm LeBlanc / Keith Morison power out of a corner.

Michael Merbach / Jeff Feldt find the rut in the snow.

Sno*Drift Rally - Results

Position O	C	Class	Car #	Driver / Co-Driver	Car	Times H:M:S
1	1	O	20	Andrew Comrie-Picard / Rod Hendricksen	Mitsubishi Evo 4	2:39:06
2	2	O	199	Travis Pastrana / Christian Edstrom	Subaru Impreza WRX	2:40:17
3	1	PGT	429	Tanner Foust / Scott Crouch	Subaru WRX	2:40:37
4	3	O	43	Ken Block / Alessandro Gelsomino	Subaru Impreza WRX	2:41:50
5	4	O	44	Henry Krolikowski / Cindy Krolikowski	Subaru WRX STi	2:46:49
6	2	PGT	59	Patrick Moro / Pamela McGarvey	Subaru WRX	2:49:32
7	5	O	27	Chris Gilligan / Joe Peterson	Mitsubishi Evo IV	2:53:44
8	3	PGT	153	Eric Langbein / Jeremy Wimpey	Subaru WRX	2:54:17
9	1	GN	606	Andrew Pinker / Robbie Durant	Subaru WRX STi	2:59:06
10	4	PGT	133	Tom Young / Jim LeBeau	Subaru WRX	3:01:12
11	5	PGT	616	Norman LeBlanc / Keith Morison	Subaru WRX Impreza	3:04:00
12	6	PGT	67	Bryan Pepp / Jerry Stang	Subaru WRX	3:04:24
13	7	PGT	93	Bob Olson / Ryan Johnson	Subaru WRX	3:05:09
14	8	PGT	12	Wojciech Okula / Adam Pelc	Subaru Impreza WRX	3:07:21
15	1	P	98	Michael Merbach / Jeff Feldt	VW Jetta	3:13:24
16	1	G5	42	Eric Burmeister / Dave Shindle	Mazda Protege	3:14:24
17	2	P	491	Jim Stevens / Marianne Stevens	Suzuki Swift GT	3:21:34
18	2	G5	72	Jon Hamilton / Ken Sabo	VW Golf TDI	3:34:33
19	1	G2	169	Eric Duncan / Matt Duncan	Honda Civic CX	4:01:06
		P	49	Sans Thompson / Craig Marr	Dodge Neon	DNF
		O	987	Peter Reilly / Phil Assad	VW Golf	DNF
		PGT	16	Kazimierz Pudelek / Mariusz Malik	Subaru Impreza RS	DNF
		O	10	Mark McElduff / Damian Irwin	Subaru STi	DNF
		O	18	Matt Iorio / Ole Holter	Subaru Impreza	DNF
		GN	774	Otis Dimiters / Alan Ockwell	Subaru WRX STi	DNF
		O	77	Alfredo DeDominicis / Mike Rossey	Mitsubishi Evo 7	DNF

Regional Rally Entrants

64	Robert Borowicz / Mariusz Borowicz	Subaru Impreza WRX	
84	Greg Drozd / Chris Gordon	Subaru Impreza	
535	Jake Himes / Matt Himes	Mitsubishi Eclipse	
523	Travis Hanson / Terry Hanson	Toyota Celica	
540	Tim Smigowski / Christina Smigowski	Mitsubishi Eclipse	
550	Kyle Sarasin / Stuart Sarasin	Eagle Talon	
532	David LaFavor / Robert LaFavor	Eagle Talon	
646	Erik Zenz / David Parps	Mazda 323 GTX	
598	Pete Hascher / Scott Rhoades	Honda Prelude	
548	Matt Bushore / Andy Bushore	VW Jetta	
584	Jimmy Brandt / John Aisma	VW Golf	
478	Evan Moen / Heath Nunnemacher	Acura Integra R	
500	Jim Kloosterman / Dan Kloosterman	Mazda 323	
26	Cary Kendall / Scott Friberg	Eagle Talon	
680	Greg Woodside / Tom Woodside	Dodge Shadow	
619	Joe Sladovich / Kent Gardam	VW Golf GTI	
21	Yurek Cienkosz / Lukasz Szela	Subaru Impreza RS	
480	Mike Gagnon / Bob Martin	Ford Focus ZX3	
601	Jon Miller / Tom McCabe	Nissan Sentra	
684	Adam Markut / John Nordlie	Eagle Talon TSI	
690	Carl Seidel / Jay Martineau	VW Golf GTI 16v	
744	Paul Koll / Matt Wappler	VW GTI	
624	Karen Purzycki / Bob Pierce	Ford Fiesta	
910	Ryan Haveman / Josh VanDenHeuvel	Dodge Neon SRT-4	

The Subaru Rally Team truck.

Right: Eric Burmeister / Dave Shindle clip the bank in their efforts to get past Michael Merbach / Jeff Feldt.

Joe Sladovich / Kent Gardam on their way in.

Right: Photographers prove they do have a use.

Rally in the 100 Acre Wood
Salem, Missouri
February 24–25, 2006

*Left: Ken Block / Alex Gelsomino
win 100 Acre Wood.*

*Above: Andrew Pinker / Robbie Durant on
their way to third overall.*

The 100 Acre Wood joined the Rally America National Championship schedule for the first time in 2006. Teams visited the old lumber and mining town of Salem—about 120 miles southwest of St. Louis—to compete on 108 miles of smooth gravel roads in the Ozarks.

Friday stages were located in the northeast, toward Cherryville, and provided seven stages with one service stop. On the Saturday, the teams would tackle twelve stages around Ellington in the southeast. The weather cooperated with the organizers and throughout the daylight stages stayed in the mid to high sixties.

Andrew Comrie-Picard was leading the championship after his win at Sno*Drift but had not entered 100 Acre Wood, so the leading contenders were the Subaru Rally Team of Travis Pastrana / Christian Edstrom and Ken Block / Alessandro Gelsomino. Alfredo de Dominicis (Dedo) / Max Daddoveri did not have the repairs to their usual Mitsubishi completed, so had rented a Subaru from Rocket Rally. Other Subaru entries included Matt Iorio / Ole Holter, Andrew Pinker / Robbie Durant and championship second-place holders Tanner Foust / Scott Crouch.

Chris Gilligan / Joe Petersen and George Plsek / Jeff Burmeister both entered their Mitsubishi Evos.

After Parc Exposé in Steelville, the teams were out to the stages where the Subaru Rally Team demonstrated its potential dominance—gaining a one-two for Block and Pastrana on the first three stages. Mark McElduff / Eddie Fries made a good start coming in third on the first two stages: Pandora's Box and Ollie Coleman Road. On the third stage, it was Dedo who was behind the Subaru team. As he settled into the car, he picked up more time and split the Subaru team drivers on stage 4.

At the first service, it was Block one second ahead of Pastrana with Dedo in third place ahead of McElduff.

The final three stages of the day used the same roads as the afternoon with some re-configuring. Block took the first stage from Pastrana but it was Pastrana from Block on the last two. Behind them, it was Dedo who kept the pressure on—waiting for any errors on the part of the leaders. Iorio had had turbo problems, which kept him out of the running but still managed to pick up a third fastest time on stage 6.

By the end of the night stages, Pastrana had clawed past Block and held a nine-second lead. Dedo was a full minute behind the leader with Foust and McElduff close by.

When the teams resumed on Saturday morning, it was more of the same on stage 8 (JB's De-

Richard Miller / Juanita Miller enter the regional event.

*Chris Gilligan / Joe Petersen
create a dust trail.*

mise) with Pastrana and Block dominating the field followed by Otis Dimiters / Alan Ockwell, McElduff and Pinker. But that was to change on the second stage of the day when Pastrana clipped a rock and hit several trees. The car was damaged beyond repair and Pastrana retired.

Block continued to set fastest times on stages 9 and 10. Then Dimiters put in a rush to take fastest on Down Doug's Choice, the last stage before lunch. It was enough to push him to third overall behind Block and Dedo and just five seconds behind McElduff.

The event had lost some time to its schedule due to a problem on stage 10, so the afternoon stages (11 and 12) were canceled. This gave the teams some extra service time and allowed the schedule to resume on time with stage 14—Mail Route.

With a two-minute cushion over Dedo, Block was able to relax and conserve the car. Pinker took the first two stages of the evening, with Block, Foust, Dimiters and Dedo all close behind. These five teams swapped times on each stage to the finish, with fastest times going to Dimiters then Block and finally Dedo taking two in a row.

As the cars pulled back into Salem, Block / Gelsomino held a forty-eight-second lead over de Dominicis / Daddoveri to take first overall and first Open class. Pinker / Durant had fought their way to third overall and took Group N.

Other class wins went to Foust / Crouch in Production GT class, Marty Kowalski / Matt Sawicki (Mitsubishi Eclipse) in Group 5, Kenny Bartram / Dennis Hotson (VW Beetle) in Production, Sans Thompson / Craig Marr (Dodge Neon) in Group 2.

Bruce Davis / Jimmy Brandt drive Camel's Hump at night.

Jon Hamilton / Ken Sabo in their diesel VW.

In the overall championship standings, Ken Block (34 points) was leading Tanner Foust (24) with Andrew Comrie-Picard (22) still in the top three due to his win at Sno*Drift.

Eric Burmeister / Dave Shindle at the Parc Exposé.

Sibing interview: Nathalie Richard interviews Pat Richard for TV.

Patrick Moro / Pam McGarvey cross the bridge at practice.

Rally in the 100 Acre Wood - Schedule

Stage #	First Car	Stage Name	Miles
Friday, February 24			
	14:31	Rally Start	
1	14:51	Pandora's Box	7.10
2	15:28	Ollie Coleman Road 1	3.95
3	15:42	Camel's Hump East	6.75
4	16:30	Haul Road 1	4.24
		Service	
5	18:16	Haul Road 2	4.24
6	18:50	Ollie Coleman Road 2	5.01
7	19:04	Camel's Hump West	4.31
Saturday, February 25			
8	10:01	J.B.'s Demise	4.25
9	10:16	Southern Loop	10.36
10	10:45	Scotia North	7.75
11	11:28	Down Doug's Choice	3.04
		Service	
12	13:33	Mail Route 1	5.32
13	13:49	Hill O'Doom 1	5.02
		Service	
14	15:23	Mail Route 2	5.32
15	15:39	Hill O'Doom 2	5.02
16	16:04	Bob Johnson Road	1.27
		Service	
17	17:24	Up Doug's Choice	3.23
18	18:02	Scotia South	11.87
19	18:31	TTFN	10.78
	18:44	Rally Finish	

Alfredo de Dominicis / Max Daddoveri run the gauntlet of the media.

Travis Pastrana / Christian Edstrom at full speed.

Christian Edstrom relaxes after car 199 retires.

Rally in the 100 Acre Wood - Results

O'all	Class	Class	Car #	Driver	Co-Driver	Car	Total
1	1	O	43	Ken Block	Alessandro Gelsomino	Subaru WRX STi	1:32:14.7
2	2	O	77	Alfredo De Dominicis	Max Daddoveri	Subaru Impreza	1:33:02.4
3	1	GN	606	Andrew Pinker	Robbie Durant	Subaru Impreza STi	1:34:05.0
4	3	O	774	Otis Dimiter	Alan Ockwell	Subaru WRX	1:34:53.9
5	1	PGT	429	Tanner Foust	Scott Crouch	Subaru WRX	1:34:58.9
6	4	O	27	Chris Gilligan	Joe Petersen	Mitsubishi Evo IV	1:37:13.8
7	5	O	30	George Plsek	Jeff Burmeister	Mitsubishi Evo	1:37:33.0
8	2	PGT	46	Matthew Johnson	Carl Fisher	Subaru WRX	1:38:21.7
9	6	O	18	Matt Iorio	Ole Holter	Subaru Impreza	1:38:36.8
10	3	PGT	153	Eric Langbein	Jeremy Wimpey	Subaru WRX	1:39:37.5
11	4	PGT	59	Patrick Moro	Pam McGarvey	Subaru WRX	1:40:12.5
12	2	GN	100	David Anton	Rebecca Greek	Subaru WRX STi	1:40:59.6
13	5	PGT	93	Bob Olson	Ryan Johnson	Subaru WRX	1:41:16.2
14	7	O	14	Amy BeberVanzo	Alex Kihurani	Mitsubishi Evo 8	1:45:34.9
15	1	G5	15	Marty Kowalski	Matt Sawicki	Mitsubishi Eclipse	1:47:22.3
16	8	O	111	Charles Kothe	Duffy Bowers	Subaru Impreza	1:48:18.4
17	2	G5	60	Bruce Davis	Jimmy Brandt	Dodge SRT-4	1:48:31.2
18	1	P	86	Kenny Bartram	Dennis Hotson	VW Beetle	1:51:11.9
19	1	G2	49	Sans Thompson	Craig Marr	Dodge Neon	1:51:18.3
20	3	G5	72	Jon Hamilton	Ken Sabo	VW Golf TDI	1:52:22.6
21	2	P	98	Mike Merbach	Jeff Feldt	VW Jetta	1:57:45.0
22	3	P	491	Jim Stevens	Marianne Stevens	Suzuki Swift	1:58:24.1
		G2	47	Robin Jones	Wil Sekella	VW Golf	DNF
		O	10	Mark McElduff	Eddie Fries	Subaru WRX STi	DNF
		PGT	12	Wojciech Okula	Adam Pelc	Subaru Impreza WRX	DNF
		O	199	Travis Pastrana	Christian Edstrom	Subaru WRX STi	DNF
		PGT	19	Tim Penasack	Marc Goldfarb	Subaru WRX	DNF
		O	107	Tim Paterson	John Allen	Mitsubishi Evo 8	DNF
		G5	123	Andrew Sutherland	Chrissie Beavis	Dodge SRT-4	DNF
		G5	42	Eric Burmeister	Dave Shindle	Mazda 3	DNF
		G2	169	Eric Duncan	Matt Duncan	Honda Civic CX	DNF

Regional Event Entrants

O	26	Cary Kendall	Scott Friberg	Mitsubishi Talon		
O	64	Robert Borowicz	Mariusz Borowicz	Subaru WRX		
PGT	625	Michael Wray	John Nordlie	Subaru Legacy		
G5	567	Bob Cutler	John Atsma	Porsche 911T		
G5	555	Colin McCleery	Nancy McCleery	Ford Sierra		
G2	592	Justin Pritchard	Bill Westrick	Ford Escort Mk2		
PGT	523	Travis Hanson	Terry Hanson	Toyota Celica		
G2	696	Bryan Holder	Tracy Payeur	Plymouth Neon		
O	413	Erik Schmidt	Mike Rose	Subaru Impreza		
G2	562	Brian Dondlinger	Dave Parps	Nissan Sentra SE-R		
G5	303	Roger Hull	David Hackett	Plymouth Laser		
PGT	671	Jeff Templeton	Heath Nunnemacher	Subaru Impreza		
G2	548	Matt Bushore	Andrew Bushore	VW Jetta		
G2	363	James Haas	Ryan Schell	Mazda MX-3		
G2	593	Gerardo Pin	Jack Butler	Ford Escort		
G2	602	Brian Schwanner	David Schwanner	Volkswagen GTI		
G5	701	Richard Miller	Juanita Miller	Saab 900T		
G2	492	James Stevens	Tess Rudder	Jeep Comanche		
G5	83	Mark Utecht		Ford Mustang		
G2	458	Stephen Sweet	James Paproth	VW Rabbit GTI		

Matthew Johnson / Carl Fisher takes second in PGT.

Massimo Daddoveri and Alfredo de Dominicis check out the opposition.

James Stevens / Tess Rudder blast their Jeep through the water.

Tim Paterson / John Allen make a one-wheel landing.

Cary Kendall / Scott Friberg win both regional events.

Corona Rally México
León, México
March 3–5, 2006

Left: Sébastien Loeb / Daniel Elena win round three of the championship.

Above: Ricardo Triviño / Checo Salom in local colors.

On the first weekend of March, the World Rally Championship visited the Guanajuato region for the third time. The Corona Rally México would use the same roads as previous years, with some variations in layout, to provide seventeen stages over 360 kilometers of gravel roads.

The single major difference in the route was the inclusion of a Super Special stage that was run at the raceway on the outskirts of the city each evening as the teams came back from the day's main competition.

As usual, the weather was flawless, with clear skies and high temperatures.

With some works regulars taking a year out of competition, it was the year of semi-works teams. The Citroën. team was entered by Kronos World Rally Team and the Peugeot entries came from OMV Peugeot Norway. Ford and Subaru had full works entries.

After taking an early lead, Petter Solberg / Phil Mills suffered power steering problems and, at the end of the first day, ceded first place to Sébastien Loeb / Daniel Elena. Loeb held his position for

the rest of the event with Solberg fighting close behind all the way. Third place went to Manfred Stohl / Ilka Minor.

Championship leader, Marcus Grönholm / Timo Rautiainen lost the road on the first day. He restarted on the second day with a penalty and was able to fight back to eighth place.

Entries from north of the border came from Wyeth Gubelmann / Cynthia Krolikowski in their regular Subaru WRX and John Cassidy / Erik Lee in a Peugeot 206 XS. Both teams finished the grueling event.

Xavier Pons / Carlos del Barrio in their Citroën Xsara WRC.

Wyeth Gubelmann / Cindy Krolikowski are one of the two American teams competing.

Gareth McHale / Paul Nagle from Ireland take the jump on Silao.

John Cassidy / Eric Lee drive through the village.

Henning Solberg / Cato Menkerud in their Peugeot 307.

Henning Solberg / Cato Menkerud speed through the village.

Sébastien Loeb / Daniel Elena drive through the mountains in their Citroën.

Corona Rally México Schedule

Stage #	First Car	Stage Name	Kms
Friday, March 3			
	9:00	Rally Start	
1	9:37	Ibarrilla 1	22.41
2	11:00	Guanajuato 1	28.87
3	11:51	Cubilete 1	21.61
4	14:28	Ibarrilla 2	22.41
5	15:51	Guanajuato 2	28.87
6	16:42	Cubilete 2	21.61
7	19:17	Nextel Superespecial 1	4.42
Saturday, March 4			
8	10:08	El Zauco 1	25.23
9	11:26	Duarte 1	23.75
10	12:17	Derramadero 1	23.27
11	15:10	El Zauco 2	25.23
12	16:28	Duarte 2	23.75
13	17:19	Derramadero 2	23.27
14	19:49	Nextel Superespecial 2	4.42
Sunday, March 5			
15	8:28	León	37.99
16	10:11	Silao	18.01
17	11:26	Nextel Superespecial 3	4.42
	12:30	Rally Finish	

Loris Baldacci / Dario D'Esposito take the jump sideways.

A local spectator starts the long walk home.

Right: Marcus Grönholm / Timo Rautiainen.

Luis Pérez Companc / José María Volta in their Ford Focus.

Right: Petter Solberg / Phil Mills.

Mikko Hirvonen / Jarmo Lehtinen.

Marcus Ligato / Rubén Garcia in their Mitsubishi Lancer Evo 9.

*Right: Manfred Stohl / Ika Minor would
come in third overall.*

The crowd watches Mirco Baldacci / Giovanni Agnese at the jump.

Corona Rally México - Results

POS	Car #	Driver		Co-Driver		Car	Total
1	1	Sébastien Loeb	F	Daniel Elena	MC	Citroën Xsara WRC	3:47:08.8
2	5	Petter Solberg	N	Phil Mills	GB	Subaru Impreza WRC	3:47:57.7
3	7	Manfred Stohl	A	Ika Minor	A	Peugeot 307 WRC	3:51:47.9
4	14	Daniel Sordo	E	Marc Martí	E	Citroën Xsara WRC	3:52:36.5
5	8	Henning Solberg	N	Cato Menkerud	N	Peugeot 307 WRC	3:59:44.2
6	15	Gareth MacHale	Irl	Paul Nagle	Irl	Ford Focus RS WRC 05	4:03:11.1
7	6	Chris Atkinson	Aus	Glenn MacNeall	Aus	Subaru Impreza WRC	4:07:48.3
8	3	Marcus Grönholm	Fin	Timo Rautiainen	Fin	Ford Focus RS WRC 06	4:08:53.0
9	31	Toshi Arai	J	Tony Sircombe	NZ	Subaru Impreza STI	4:09:43.4
10	39	Nasser Al-Attiyah	QAT	Chris Patterson	GB	Subaru Impreza STI	4:10:32.3
11	36	Mirco Baldacci	RSM	Giovanni Agnese	I	Mitsubishi Lancer Evo 9	4:15:32.6
12	10	Luis Pérez Companc	RA	José María Volta	RA	Ford Focus RS WRC 04	4:16:03.3
13	38	Leszek Kuzaj	PL	Maciek Szczepaniak	PL	Subaru Impreza STI	4:19:29.6
14	4	Mikko Hirvonen	Fin	Jarmo Lehtinen	Fin	Ford Focus RS WRC 06	4:23:18.9
15	42	Sergei Uspenskiy	RUS	Dimitry Eremeev	RUS	Subaru Impreza STI	4:24:30.6
16	9	Matthew Wilson	GB	Michael Orr	GB	Ford Focus RS WRC 04	4:26:57.5
17	32	Marcus Ligato	RA	Rubén García	RA	Mitsubishi Lancer Evo 9	4:32:38.1
18	43	Stepan Vojtech	CZ	Michal Ernst	CZ	Mitsubishi Lancer Evo 8	4:35:30.2
19	66	Javier Ortuño	Mex	Lorena Fuentes	Mex	Subaru Impreza STI	4:39:28.3
20	67	Peter Thomson	Can	R Hendricksen	USA	Subaru Impreza WRX	4:43:03.0
21	60	Francisco Name	Mex	Armando Zapata	Mex	Mitsubishi Lancer Evo 7	4:56:54.7
22	62	Alejandro Pimentel	Mex	Jorge Mondragón	Mex	Mitsubishi Lancer	4:56:57.1
23	63	Wyeth Gubelmann	USA	Cynthia Krolikowski	USA	Subaru Impreza STI	4:57:43.0
24	61	Loris Baldacci	RSM	Dario D'Esposito	I	Subaru Impreza STI	4:58:06.1
25	37	Jari-Matti Latvala	Fin	Mikka Anttila	Fin	Subaru Impreza STI	4:59:32.8
26	65	Benito Guerra	Mex	Jaime Lozano	Mex	Mitsubishi Lancer	5:01:02.3
27	70	Adrián Díaz Caneja	Mex	Javier Antista	Mex	Peugeot 206 XS	5:10:08.6
28	72	Mauricio Serrano	Mex	Juan Alessio-Robles	Mex	Peugeot 206 XS	5:19:06.4
29	75	Oscar Uribe F.	Mex	Oscar Uribe B.	Mex	Peugeot 206 XS	5:28:38.4
30	69	Gabriel Beltrán	ROU	Felipe Guelfi	ROU	Peugeot 206 XS	5:33:43.5
31	68	Omar Chávez	Mex	Luis Arciga	Mex	Peugeot 206 XS	5:35:35.1
32	71	John Cassidy	USA	Erik Lee	USA	Peugeot 206 XS	5:42:21.5
33	73	Roberto Gnecchi	Mex	Jorge Mora	Mex	Peugeot 206 XS	5:49:00.7
	2	Xavier Pons	E	Carlos del Barrio	E	Citroën Xsara WRC	DNF
	16	Ricardo Triviño	Mex	Checo Salom	E	Peugeot 206 WRC	DNF
	33	Fumio Nutahara	J	Daniel Barritt	GB	Mitsubishi Lancer Evo 9	DNF
	34	Sebastián Beltrán	RA	Ricardo Rojas	RCH	Mitsubishi Lancer Evo 9	DNF
	35	Gabriel Pozzo	RA	Daniel Stillo	RA	Mitsubishi Lancer Evo 9	DNF
	74	Luis Armando Rodrígu	Mex	Fabian Islas	Mex	Peugeot 206 XS	DNF

Daniel Sordo / Marc Marti and their Citroën.

Petter Solberg / Phil Mills place second overall.

Marcus Grönholm / Timo Rautiainen raise a dust trail.

Rally New York USA
Monticello, New York
April 7–8, 2006

Tom Lawless / Graham Quinn win Rally New York.

Left: Jeremy Drislane / Carl Williamson.

It was a cool and damp weekend for the first visit of the year to Monticello. This free-wheeling town, near the location of the Woodstock Festival, would be home-for-the-weekend of the first U.S. Rally Championship event of the year.

For the first time, the event would be run as an all-asphalt affair. While this might simplify the competitor's planning—no need for gravel tires—it forced the organizers to limit their selection of roads and plan a compact route that used some roads multiple times.

On Friday, the competition would use the fast hilly roads around Liberty. Saturday morning was centered in Narrowsburg including the crowd's favorite—Blind Pond —before returning to Liberty for the afternoon session and finish. To reduce speeds on some of the fastest stretches of road, chicanes made from barrels and tape were placed strategically. The competitors would be penalized ten seconds for each chicane they hit. As they had not seen the chicanes during the practice day, it was sure that many teams would touch barrels.

Enda McCormack / Mark McAllister land hard after the jump . . .

Patrick Brennan and Sean Moriarty work late to get ready for the event.

There was a strong entry of forty-nine cars although only seventeen had entered for the full national championship event, the rest were competing in the two single-day regional events. Top of the entry list were the two Mitsubishis of Tom Lawless / Graham Quinn and Seamus Burke / Chrissie Beavis. Burke had won this event last year and Lawless won the IRNY on similar roads just six months before. Behind them on the road the teams included Matt Iorio / Jeremy Wimpey (Subaru) and Otis Dimiters / Alan Ockwell (Subaru).

Most of the Friday stages were taken in a consistent rain but by Saturday the showers had passed and the roads dried out.

The first stage—the sixteen miles of Benton Hollow—saw Burke come in a full twenty-five seconds ahead of Lawless, who had chosen to run on dry tires. David Anton / Robbie Durant took third with Dimiters fourth.

On the second stage Burke consolidated his

. . . and finish their rally on the water.

lead, though only by a further four seconds, then Lawless came back by four seconds. The final stage of the day was taken by Jeremy Drislane / Carl Williamson (Mitsubishi) with Lawless and Burke within four seconds.

As the teams came back to Monticello for the night, Burke had maintained his lead over Lawless, with Anton and Drislane lying third and fourth.

The Saturday morning stages saw the fight between Burke and Lawless continue as they traded fastest times through the Narrowsburg stages. Drislane, Dimiters and Anton were always in contention with Drislane taking fastest time on the first running of Blind Pond.

When the crews came round to Blind Pond again, it provided more excitement than they had planned for Enda McCormack / Mark McAllister when they took the jump at full speed and bounced into the pond. The stage was canceled although both driver and co-driver were fine.

Otis Dimiters / Alan Ockwell.

Jeremy Drislane / Carl Williamson take the jump on their way to third overall.

By the lunchtime service, Burke was still maintaining that twenty-second lead over Lawless with Drislane in third.

The final four stages continued the fight with stages going to Burke, Lawless, Burke, Lawless. Lawless was gradually catching Burke a second at a time. Drislane took third on all four stages with Anton and Dimiters close behind.

As the teams pulled into the finish celebrations at Liberty it looked like Burke had taken the event by a mere seven seconds—until the road penalties for the chicanes were added. Lawless had hit one fewer chicane than Burke, giving him ten seconds fewer penalties and putting him ahead of Burke by just three seconds. Lawless /

Below: Dan Brosnan / Paddy McCague win Modified 2 Class.

Quinn won the event over Burke / Beavis. Third place and the Group N class win went to Anton / Durant. Iorio / Wimpey were rewarded for a consistent run with fourth place.

Other class winners were Mark Lawrence / Robert Maciejski in their Open Two-Wheel VW Golf and Brian Street / David Weiman in their Super Stock Toyota Celica.

Above: Michael Cosgrove / John O'Reilly.

Rally New York - Schedule

Stage #	First Car	Stage Name	Miles
Friday, April 7			
	12:15	Rally Start - Monticello	
1	12:42	Benton Hollow 1	16.60
2	13:14	East Hill 1	4.85
3	13:54	Benton Hollow 2	16.60
		Service - Monticello Airport	
4	16:31	Benton Hollow 3	16.60
5	17:03	East Hill 2	4.85
		Service - Monticello Airport	
Saturday, April 8			
6	8:41	Mathias Weiden East 1	4.29
7	8:56	Blind Pond 1	5.43
		Service - Narrowsburg	
8	9:58	Mathias Weiden East 2	4.29
9	10:13	Blind Pond 2	5.43
		Service - Narrowsburg	
10	11:15	Mathias Weiden East 3	4.29
11	11:30	Blind Pond 3	5.43
		Service - Monticello Airport	
12	14:04	Monticello Airport	0.62
13	14:49	Cutler 1	5.00
14	15:10	Midway 1	16.53
		Service - Monticello Airport	
15	17:40	Cutler 2	5.00
16	18:01	Midway 2	16.53
	18:45	Rally Finish - Liberty	

Right: Seamus Burke / Chrissie Beavis place second overall.

Left: Martin Egan / Tommy Byrne compete in a Toyota Corolla.

Rally New York - Results

O'All	Class	Class	Car #	Driver	Co-Driver	Car	Total MM:SS
1	1	O4	1	Tom Lawless	Graham Quinn	Mitsubishi Evo 8	89:58
2	2	O4	2	Seamus Burke	Chrissie Beavis	Mitsubishi Evo	90:01
3	1	P1	9	Jeremy Drislane	Carl Williamson	Mitsubishi Evo 4	92:22
4	1	GN	8	David Anton	Robbie Durant	Subaru WRX STI	94:25
5	3	O4	3	Matt Iorio	Jeremy Wimpey	Subaru Impreza	96:45
6	2	P1	19	Patrick Brennan	Sean Moriarty	Subaru WRX STI	96:54
7	4	O4	10	Daniel O'Brien	Stephen Duffy	Subaru STI	97:50
8	5	O4	12	Brian Scott	John Dillon	Subaru WRX STI	99:08
9	1	SS	18	Emilio Arce	Sarah Gardescu	Subaru Impreza	102:25
10	3	P1	13	Darrell Pugh	Jonathan Barnes	Mitsubishi Eclipse	102:58
11	2	GN	6	Otis Dimiters	Alan Ockwell	Subaru WRX STI	104:38
12	2	SS	27	Donal McGivney	Noel Gallagher	Subaru WRX STI	105:33
13	1	O2	31	Mark Lawrence	Robert Maciejski	VW Golf	107:27
14	2	O2	33	Eric Burmeister	Dave Shindle	Mazda 3	107:43
15	1	M2	24	Dan Brosnan	Paddy McCague	Nissan Sentra	110:46
16	3	SS	38	Seamus McKiernan	Martin Shekleton	Eagle Talon AWD	111:27
17	6	O4	39	George Georgakopoulos	Faruq Mays	Subaru Impreza	113:20
18	2	M2	36	Andrew Frick	Simon Wright	VW Scirocco	113:44
19	3	O2	32	Bruce Davis	Jimmy Brandt	Dodge Neon SRT-4	113:53
19	1	P2	40	Per Schroeder	Jason Grahn	Subaru Impreza	113:53
21	4	SS	29	Michael Cosgrove	John O'Reilly	Mitsubishi Eclipse	114:51
22	3	M2	44	David Furey	Brian Heneghan	VW GTI	115:18
23	2	P2	45	Alex Kuhner	Peter Monin	Subaru Impreza	115:43
24	4	P1	26	Marcelo Zuleta	Merida Johnny	Subaru WRX	124:57
25	7	O4	17	Gerard Coffey	David Dooley	Mitsubishi Evo 8	130:03
26	5	SS	42	Brian Street	David Weiman	Toyota Celica	131:38
27	4	M2	37	Larry Duane	Eamon Sweeney	Toyota Corolla	134:28
28	1	S	49	Ronald Vecchioni	Levi Magyar	Mazda RX-7	147:50
29	5	P1	16	Enda McCormack	Mark McAllister	Mitsubishi Evo 6	361:04
30	6	P1	14	Maciej Przybysz	Dominik Jozwiak	Subaru Impreza	377:24
31	5	SS	20	Martin O'Flynn	Bernie Obry	Mitsubishi Eclipse	381:49
		M2	48	Joao Ferreira	Niall Johnson	VW GTI	DNF
		S	47	John Arango	William Doyle	BMW 325i	DNF
		SS	43	Craig Studnicky	Jeffrey Hagan	Toyota Celica	DNF
		M2	41	Martin Egan	Tommy Byrne	Toyota Corolla	DNF
		P1	23	Andrew Hadjiminas	Alex Kihurani	Subaru Impreza	DNF
		O4	7	Charlie Donnelly	Barry McCann	Mitsubishi Evo 2	DNF
		P2	46	Brian Rutledge	Declan Brady	Subaru Impreza	DNF
		M1	34	Michael Hall	Dave Stockdill	Mitsu Mighty Max	DNF
		O4	5	Patrick Farrell	Bernard Farrell	Subaru Impreza	DNF
		M2	25	Colin Bombara	Larry Duva	Dodge Neon	DNF
		SS	21	Hampton Bridwell	Joshua Katinger	Toyota Celica	DNF

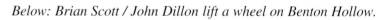

Per Schroeder / Jason Grahn win P2 in the Grassroots Motorsports project car.

Below: Brian Scott / John Dillon lift a wheel on Benton Hollow.

Tom Lawless discusses the event with Olga Orisek (L) and Aileen Gunther, a member of the New York State Assembly.

Andrew Frick / Simon Wright enter a Volkswagen Scirocco.

David Anton / Robbie Durant take their Subaru to fourth overall.

John Arango / William Doyle would not finish the course in their BMW.

Oregon Trail Rally
Hillsboro, Oregon
April 21–23, 2006

Left: Alfredo de Dominicis / Massimo Daddoveri entertain the crowds.

Andrew Pinker / Robbie Durant win the event.

Oregon hosted the third round of the Rally America Series from their regular home of Hillsboro, on the edge of the Portland metropolitan area.

The organizers had received fifty-six entries with over twenty competing at the national championship level.

The entry list was led by the Subaru Rally Team entries of Travis Pastrana / Christian Edstrom and Ken Block / Alex Gelsomino. The top ten seeded positions were dominated by Subaru with further entries from Matt Iorio / Ole Holter and Andrew Pinker / Robbie Durant. The only non-Subaru in the top ten was the lone Mitsubishi of Alfredo de Dominicis (Dedo) / Massimo Daddoveri. Further down the field, the crowd-pleasers included the Audi Quattro entered by Victor Bartosek / Don Flagg, the GMC Sonoma from Joshua Milos / Michael Milos and Kenny Bartram / Dennis Hotson in a VW Beetle.

As usual, the event started with an evening of Super Special stage rallying using the access roads of the Portland International Speedway. There were six stages totaling 10.4 miles. By the end of

Kim DeMotte takes time to check the road book.

Rick Schmeling / Richard Kasten win Group 5 in the first regional day event.

the evening Pinker was leading with a time of 11:12 followed, just two seconds behind by Pastrana then Block and Iorio. With less than a minute separating the top ten, it was all to play for in the woods over the rest of the weekend.

The Saturday stages were held fifty miles west of Hillsboro in the Tillamook State Forest. The first stage of the day, On the Lookout, would bring the teams deep into the forest where they would use the roads of Bark Shanty and Murphy Camp for morning and afternoon competition.

Pinker set fastest time on On the Lookout followed by Block and Pastrana. At almost twenty miles, stage 8, Bark Shanty Long, would be the longest stage of the event. It was taken by Pinker from Pastrana and Iorio. Pinker went on to make it a clean sweep of the morning stages when he took East to South from Pastrana and Dedo.

By lunch Pinker had built a fifty-second lead over Pastrana and Block, despite having to run first on the road and clear the stones.

On the afternoon pass of the roads, Pinker took fastest time twice and Iorio came in first on the final stage. Pastrana and Block were both following the team goal of the overall championship, and drove consistently to be in the top five on every stage. By the time the crews came back to Hillsboro at the end of the day, Pinker led from Pastrana and Block with Iorio in fourth place. Leading PGT class were Eric Langbein / Jeremy Wimpey and Group N was led by Wyeth Gubelmann / Cynthia Krolikowski.

The Sunday would be centered north west of Hillsboro at Vernonia. The Emerald Forest stage would be run twice before lunch then the teams would make two laps of South Louie and Scotty's Jig.

Iorio took fastest time on the first running of Emerald Forest, then Block and Pinker. Second time through, it was Block followed by Pastrana and Pinker.

Through the afternoon stages it was Pinker who maintained his advantage, coming second on both passes of South Louie from Block and Dedo, and taking fastest time on both runs through Scotty's Jig. As the afternoon wore on Norm LeBlanc / Keith Morison and Matthew Johnson / Kim DeMotte both started to put up times that got them into the top five on stages.

The final result was a clear victory for Pinker / Durant, who had established a lead on the first day and stayed in front throughout. The Subaru Rally Team achieved their goal of building their championship points with solid second and third places. Pastrana was just one minute forty seconds behind Pinker with Block a further forty seconds adrift. De Dominicis / Daddoveri were fourth with Johnson / DeMotte in fifth and first in PGT class. Gubelmann / Krolikowski took Group N and Chip Miller / Kathryn Hansen took Group 2 in their Honda Civic. The Group 5 result went to Bruce

Above: Scott Kovalik / Karen Wagner run in PGT class.

Below: Gary Cavett / Alan Perry win the first regional event.

Cars line up at Parc Exposé.

Davis / Jimmy Brandt in their Dodge Neon and Bartram / Hotson took Production.

After three events, Block was leading the championship with 48 points from Pinker (40) and Pastrana (35).

Ken Block and Travis Pastrana with Christian Edstrom plan their event.

Below: Eric Duncan / Matt Duncan place second in Group 2.

Sans Thompson.

Oregon Trail Rally - Schedule

Stage #	First Car	Stage Name	Miles
Friday, April 21			
	15:00	Rally Start - Portland Intl	
Raceway			
1	16:21	Armco Trail 1	1.84
2	16:44	Northwest Passage 1	1.92
3	17:07	Armco Trail 2	1.84
4	17:30	Northwest Passage 2	1.92
5	19:08	PIR Land Rush	0.88
6	20:06	Light the Way	2.00
Saturday, April 22			
7	11:33	On the Lookout	5.00
		Service - Trask	
8	12:35	Bark Shanty Long	19.68
9	13:25	East to South	6.99
		Service - Trask	
10	14:45	Bobcat	6.40
		Service - Trask	
11	15:49	Bark Shanty	10.90
12	16:22	Murphy Camp	7.26
Sunday, April 23			
13	9:53	Emerald Forest 1	9.51
		Service - Vernonia	
14	11:52	Emerald Forest 2	9.51
		Service - Vernonia	
15	13:36	South Louie 1	10.03
16	14:05	Scotty's Jig 1	9.71
		Service - Vernonia	
17	16:09	South Louie 2	10.03
18	16:38	Scotty's Jig 2	9.71
	17:50	Rally Finish - Hillsboro	

Eric Logue / William Beers pass the
slow-rolled Subaru of Joan
Hoskinson / Jeff Secor.

Travis Pastrana / Christian Edstrom are second overall.

Paul Eklund / Jeff Price come out of the forests.

Oregon Trail Rally - Results

POSITION O'all	Class	Class	Car #	Driver	Co-Driver	Car	Total H:MM:SS.D
1	1	O	606	Andrew Pinker	Robbie Durant	Subaru Impreza STi	2:25:21.8
2	2	O	199	Travis Pastrana	Christian Edstrom	Subaru Impreza WRX STi	2:27:02.2
3	3	O	43	Ken Block	Alex Gelsomino	Subaru Impreza WRX STi	2:27:46.5
4	4	O	77	Alfredo De Dominicis	Massimo Daddoveri	Mitsubishi Evo 7	2:31:46.2
5	1	PGT	46	Matthew Johnson	Kim DeMotte	Subaru WRX	2:33:07.8
6	1	GN	103	Wyeth Gubelmann	Cynthia Krolikowski	Subaru STi	2:34:01.3
7	2	PGT	153	Eric Langbein	Jeremy Wimpey	Subaru WRX	2:34:44.5
8	5	O	288	Gary Cavett	Alan Perry	Subaru Impreza	2:35:31.5
9	3	PGT	616	Norm LeBlanc	Keith Morison	Subaru WRX	2:36:33.2
10	2	GN	22	Ralph Kosmides	John Dillon	Subaru WRX	2:39:27.4
11	6	O	14	Amy BeberVanzo	Alex Kihurani	Mitsubishi Evo 8	2:47:27.1
12	1	G2	247	Chip Miller	Kathryn Hansen	Honda Civic	2:57:17.3
13	1	G5	60	Bruce Davis	Jimmy Brandt	Dodge Neon SRT-4	2:59:34.8
14	1	P	86	Kenny Bartram	Dennis Hotson	VW Beetle	3:05:39.4
15	2	G2	169	Eric Duncan	Matt Duncan	Honda Civic	3:15:49.6
16	3	G2	473	Lars Wolfe	Scot Langford	VW	3:38:49.1
		PGT	82	Joan Hoskinson	Jeff Secor	Subaru Impreza RS	DNF
		O	18	Matt Iorio	Ole Holter	Subaru Impreza	DNF
		PGT	59	Patrick Moro	Mike Rossey	Subaru WRX	DNF
		O	10	Mark McElduff	Patrick Walsh	Subaru WRX STi	DNF
		O	107	Tim Paterson	John Allen	Mitsubishi Evo 8	DNF
		G5	26	Cary Kendall	Scott Friberg	Dodge SRT-4	DNF
		G2	49	Sans Thompson	Craig Marr	Dodge Neon	DNF
		PGT	93	Bob Olson	Ryan Johnson	Subaru WRX	DNF

Regional Event Entrants

	Class	Car #	Driver	Co-Driver	Car
	O	207	Dave Hintz	Rick Hintz	Subaru WRX
	O	233	Paul Eklund	Jeff Price	Subaru WRX STi
	O	413	Erik Schmidt	Grant Hughes	Subaru Impreza
	O	252	Bob Trinder	Paul Westwick	Subaru WRX
	O	275	Nat Stow	Ben Bradley	Subaru
	O	297	Steve Greer	Kelly Greer	Subaru Impreza
	PGT	215	Jamie Thomas	Matthew Gauger	Subaru WRX Wagon
	PGT	285	Mike Goodwin	Debbie Wenzara	Subaru Impreza WRX
	G2	437	Tom Burress	Dan Burress	VW Rabbit
	O	294	Barrett Dash	Jason Grahn	Subaru STi
	G5	277	Rick Schmeling	Richard Kasten	Mazda RX7
	O	424	Mark Mager	Jody Olson	Subaru Legacy
	O	438	Victor Bartosek	Don Flagg	Audi UR Quattro
	G2	298	James Thomson	Tim Hollenbeck	VW Golf
	P	258	Kris Dahl	K Edward Dahl	Acura Integra
	P	649	Cody Crane	Brandon Buck	Honda CRX
	O	447	Christopher Baldini	COdy Konda	Mazda 323 GTX
	O	436	Adam Ullevig	Eric Bolton	Subaru Impreza
	O	335	Jay Woodward	Tracy Manspeaker	Mazda 323 GTX
	PGT	486	Martin Menning	Ryan Schnell	Subaru Impreza
	G5	295	Charles Buren	Teresa Holem	Subaru Impreza
	G5	206	Joshua Milos	Michael Milos	GMC Sonoma
	G2	404	Alex Needham	Bryce Reinhardt	Nissan Sentra
	P	132	April Smith	Jeffrey Zurschmeide	Geo Metro
	G5	768	Kala Rounds	Shadd Foster	Mazda RX3
	G2	652	Eric Logue	William Beers	VW Rabbit
	PGT	502	Matthew Milner	John Taylor	Subaru Legacy
	G2	464	Stevan Arychuk	Tina Warner	VW GTI
	PGT	454	Scott Kovalik	Karen Wagner	Eagle Talon TSi
	PGT	714	Roger Dauffenbach	Tim Sardelich	Subaru WRX
	O	376	Blake Yoon	Chrissie Beavis	Subaru WRX
	PGT	93	Bob Olson	Ryan Johnson	Subaru WRX

Ben Bradley.

Right: Ken Block / Alex Gelsomino lift a wheel on their way to third overall.

Ralph Kosmides / John Dillon at the hairpin on Bark Shanty.

Matt Iorio / Ole Holter relax at the service area.

SUBARU
RIM OF THE WORLD RALLY

Subaru
Rim of the World Rally
Lancaster, California
April 28–29, 2006

For round two of the U.S. Rally Championship, the action moved to the West Coast and the regular home of the Rim of the World—Lancaster, California.

Unlike last year's stormy weather, the teams were greeted by clear blue skies with highs in the seventies and sun all the way.

For two days of competition, the teams would be based at the Antelope Valley Fairgrounds, which would also provide spectators with the opportunity to watch the cars in action over three Super Special stages. The fairgrounds would also host an exhibition of tuner parts and equipment and a drifting competition.

Away from the fairgrounds, the teams would compete in the Angeles National Forest. On Friday, there would be twenty-four miles of night stages running along the crests of Magic Mountain and Mount Gleason. Saturday would start with a double run along Del Sur in the morning followed by two loops of stages along the Leona Valley. In all, the forty-nine entries would cover ninety-five stage miles.

Entries were led by the Subaru Rally Team. Travis Pastrana had a new (to him) co-driver with Jakke Honkanen taking the seat for one event. Ken Block was co-driven by his usual partner Alex

Left: George Georgakopoulos / Faruq Mays at the fairgrounds.

Above: Travis Pastrana (co-driven by Jakke Honkanen) got his first U.S. national win.

Jeff Rados / Guido Hamacher use all the road in their Ford Ranger.

Scott Clark / Tamara Clark get a surprise when they land their Subaru.

Gelsomino. Behind the Subarus were a trio of Mitsubishis: George Plsek / Jeff Burmeister, Leon Styles / Mark McAllister and Wolfgang Hoeck / Piers O'Hanlon.

Friday consisted of four stages starting with the first run of the Super Special. Teams were started in tandem and the organizers had been particularly devious as the stage started with a high jump. Whichever team came out the jump first could dominate the other team round the rest of the course as the dust was flying high. The trucks of Chad Dykes / Bill Graham and Jeff Rados / Guido Hamacher got a lot of air—and a lot of support from the crowd but it was Pastrana who took fastest time from Plsek then Block.

Through the night stages it was the Subarus that would build a lead with Pastrana taking Mount Gleason and Magic Mountain. The third stage, Messenger Flats, went to Block from Pastrana. Styles, Plsek and Brian Scott / John Dillon were never far behind. Hoeck lost twenty minutes on stage 3 putting him out of contention for the event.

As the cars came into Lancaster at the end of the day's competition, Pastrana led the field fewer than thirty seconds ahead of Block, who had one minute over Plsek then Scott.

On Saturday morning, Pastrana increased his lead with a double win on the two runnings of Del Sur, taking the honors from Block. On the first run through, Blake Yoon / Nathalie Richard got third fastest ahead of Styles, later it was Styles from Plsek.

The afternoon started with the second run of the Super Special, which was taken by Block. He went on to take the next two stages in the forests, beating Pastrana then Plsek and Styles, and closing to within twenty-nine seconds of Pastrana. But Pastrana came back on the final stage of the afternoon and then held his lead over the evening stages—taking them all from Block in second place and Plsek in third.

Thus Pastrana, with co-driver Honkanen, won his first gravel rally beating team mates Block / Gelsomino by a margin of 1.3 minutes. Third, and three minutes back, were Plsek / Burmeister then Styles / McAllister.

Other class wins went to Dennis Chizma / Andrew Cushman (Porsche 964) in Super Stock, Bruce Davis / Jimmy Brandt (Dodge Neon) in Open 2WD and Cem Akdeniz / Mustafa Samli (Subaru Impreza) in Group N.

Right, above: Dennis Chizma / Andrew Cushman win Super Stock.

Right, below: George Plsek / Jeff Burmeister take third overall.

Spectators in the California desert.

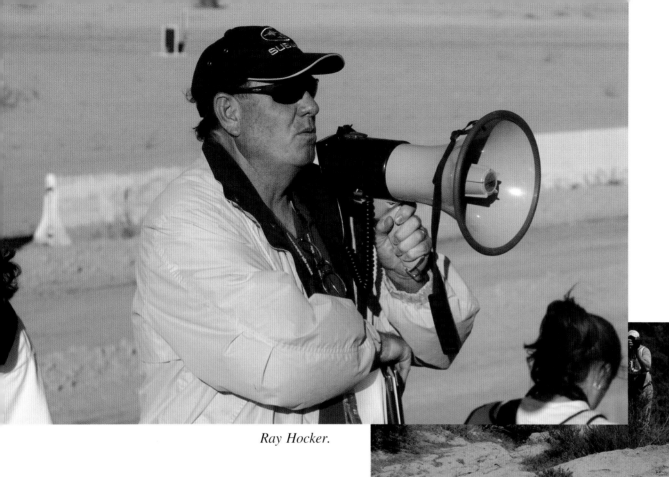

Ray Hocker.

Dave Coleman / Amar Sehmi in the Sport Compact Car *magazine project car.*

Subaru Rim of the World Rally - Schedule

Stage #	First Car	Stage Name	Miles
Friday, April 28			
	18:58	Rally Start - AVFG	
1	19:08	Antelope Valley Fairground	1.0
2	20:01	Mount Gleason	6.5
3	20:41	Messenger Flats West	9.1
4	21:26	Magic Mountain West	8.7
Saturday, April 29			
5	8:48	Del Sur South	9.1
6	10:21	Del Sur North	9.1
		Service - AVFG	
7	12:29	Antelope Valley Fairground	1.0
8	13:12	Leona West	9.2
9	14:55	Liebre Mountain 1	11.5
10	15:33	Maxwell Road 1	8.6
		Service - AVFG	
11	17:34	Antelope Valley Fairground	1.0
12	18:52	Liebre Mountain 2	11.5
13	19:30	Maxwell Road 2	8.6
	20:40	Rally Finish - AVFG	

Lisa Klassen / Marie Chizma take on the fairgrounds at night.

Below: Teams attend the driver briefing.

Wolfgang Hoeck / Piers O'Hanlon.

Tanner Foust.

Below: George Plsek / Jeff Burmeister.

Above: Blake Yoon / Nathalie Richard.

Below: Travis Pastrana.

*Right: Paul Williamson / Travis Bos
attack the Leona Valley stage.*

*Travis Pastrana / Jakke Honkan lead Ken
Block / Alex Gelsomino into the jump.*

Tsukasa Gushi / Ken Gushi would repair their Subaru in time to continue the rally.

Tony Chavez / Doug Robinson would retire after four stages.

Subaru Rim of the World Rally - Results

POSITION O'all	Class	Class	Car #	Driver	Co-Driver	Car	Total MMM.DD
1	1	04	199	Travis Pastrana	Jakke Honkanen	Subaru WRX STi	130.87
2	2	04	43	Ken Block	Alex Gelsomino	Subaru WRX STi	132.16
3	3	04	30	George Plsek	Jeff Burmeister	Mitsubishi Lancer Evo	135.46
4	4	04	374	Leon Styles	Mark McAllister	Mitsubishi Lancer Evo	138.33
5	5	04	360	Randy Dowell	Jonathan Schiller	Mitsubishi Mirage	142.09
6	1	SS	165	Dennis Chizma	Andrew Cushman	Porsche 964-C4	147.46
7	1	02	60	Bruce Davis	Jimmy Brandt	Dodge Neon SRT-4	153.91
8	6	04	88	George Georgakopoulos	Faruq Mays	Subaru WRX STi	154.54
9	2	02	418	Jimmy Keeney	Brian Moody	Honda Civic	154.70
10	1	GN	474	Cem Akdeniz	Mustafa Samil	Subaru Impreza STi	158.82
11	7	04	89	Wolfgang Hoeck	Piers O'Hanlon	Mitsubishi Lancer Evo	171.20
12	1	S	761	Kristopher Marciniak	Christine Wittish	Dodge Neon	177.60
		04	14	Amy BeberVanzo	Alexander Kihurani	Mitsubishi	DNF
		04	96	Brian Scott	John Dillon	Subaru WRX STi	DNF
		04	127	Chad Dykes	Billy Graham	Chevy S10	DNF
		02	301	Tony Chavez	Doug Robinson	VW Golf	DNF
		04	376	Blake Yoon	Nathalie Richard	Mitsubishi Evo 7	DNF

Regional Event Entrants

PGT	262	Dan Brink	Vern Anderson	Eagle Talon
G2	792	George Doganis	Tom Smith	Nissan Sentra SE-R
G5	674	Jeff Rados	Guido Hamacher	Ford Ranger
G2	301	Tony Chavez	Doug Robinson	VW Golf
04	829	Tsukasa Gushi	Ken Gushi	Subaru WRX
PGT	368	Marvin Ronquillo	John Burke	Subaru WRX
04	318	Vartan Samuelian	L Babahikian	Mitsubishi
G2	695	Larry Gross	Doug Young	Toyota Corolla
G2	737	Sarkis Mazmanian	M Mazmanian	Acura Integra
G2	691	Jeremy Fry	Clay Cullen	Toyota Corolla
PGT	354	Robert Brinkhurst	Mat Stokes	Subaru Legacy
G2	328	Tony Dela Cuesta	JD Recto	Toyota Trueno
G2	355	Ricardo Lozada	T Stonecipher	Toyota Corolla
G2	725	Dave Carapetyan	Justin Kwak	Acura Integra
G5	776	Lisa Klassen	C Marie Chizma	Toyota Corolla
PGT	369	Paul Willemsen	Travis Bos	Mitsubishi Eclipse GSX
G5	632	Dean Schlingmann	Chip Doeden	Suzuki Reno
G5	321	Murat Okcuoglu	Burak Tuglu	Mitsubishi Starion
P	300	Patrick Rodi	Bret Robinson	Mazda RX-7
04	334	Neil Bliss	Mike Warfield	Subaru WRX
PGT	666	Joanna Balsamo	Sean McElwain	Subaru WRX
PGT	777	Bristol Keele	George Scott	Subaru Impreza
G2	446	J Imai	Sameer Parekh	Suzuki Swift GT
04	39	Scott Clark	Tamara Clark	Subaru
G5	314	Jun Andrada	Alan Marasigan	Toyota Corolla
G2	406	Rem Wyatt	Pamela Wyatt	VW Golf
04	344	Hakan Okcuoglu	Cengiz Nomer	Mitsubishi Eclipse
04	340	Chrissie Beavis	Amy Trowbridge	Subaru WRX
G2	346	Dave Coleman	Amar Sehmi	Datsun 510
04	322	Bob Pendergrass	H Sheldon	Chevy Blazer
G2	318	Matt Johnston	Ian Pinter	Toyota Starlet

A family affair for George Plsek.

Ken Block / Alex Gelsomino and Leon Styles / Mark McAllister jump at the fairgrounds.

Tanner Foust takes time off from rally competition to demonstrate drifting.

Olympus Rally

OLYMPUS RALLY
Washington's round of the USRC
2006

Olympus Rally
Shelton, Washington
May 20–21, 2006

The third round of the U.S. Rally Championship would be the Olympus Rally, returning to Washington state after an absence of almost twenty years. The event was based in Shelton just outside Olympia, Washington.

After two rounds of the championship, it was close scoring on the leaderboard with Travis Pastrana and Tom Lawless sharing the lead with thirty-six points apiece and George Georgakopoulos just one point behind. Neither Pastrana nor Lawless were entered, so the weekend was likely to make a new leader.

The two-day national event was using the same roads as the two regional one-day events. So while the overall entry was good, the national championship entry was eleven. Top competitors in open class included Wolfgang Hoeck / Piers O'Hanlon and Blake Yoon / Nathalie Richard in their Mitsubishi Evos, Gary Cavett / Jeff Secor, Wyeth Gubelmann / Cindy Krolikowski and Ralph Kosmides / Alan Ockwell had entered Subaru Imprezas.

The top two-wheel drive entry was from Bruce Davis / Jimmy Brandt, while "special attractions"

Above: Cars assemble at Parc Exposé in Washington's capital.

Left: Wyeth Gubelmann / Cindy Krolikowski take first place.

Blake Yoon / Nathalie Richard are fastest on the second day.

Below: Co-drivers do their preparation.

came from Leon Styles / Lisa Klassen in their Ford Escort Mk2 and Garth Ankeny / Russ Kraushaar in an immaculate Saab 96.

After Parc Exposé at the state capital, Friday stages were to the southwest of Shelton. Before he had a chance to settle into the event, just a mile into Summit Loop, Yoon high-centered and lost twenty-two minutes before being pulled out by Styles. It was Gubelmann who took advantage and set fastest time ahead of Kosmides and Hoeck.

On stage 2, Maxwell Loop, Yoon came back to take second behind Gubelmann. Then, on the ORV Super Special, it was the local team of Dave Hintz / Rick Hintz who took fastest time over Yoon and Cavett. Hintz's good performance would also be his final stage as he had to retire with a blown engine.

The early afternoon would see the first three stages repeated. Gubelmann took Summit Loop for the second time before Yoon started a streak of four stage wins—Maxwell Loop and ORV before service, then Wildcat and Skookum after service. Behind him, the fight was between Gubelmann, Kosmides and Hoeck, who took the last two stages of the day. Stage 5 would see the retirement of George Georgakopoulos / Faruq Mays who had had two off-road excursions by that time.

By the end of day one it was Gubelmann in the lead. He had taken fastest time on the first stage of the day and held it through every stage. Behind him came Kosmides, then Cavett and Hoeck.

The second day's stages would be to the west of Shelton—two loops round Stillwater, Cougar Meadow and Nahwatzel (at almost twenty miles, the sting in the tail of the event).

Todd Lengacher / Merrilee Gilley would not make it far in their popular Audi.

Ralph Kosmides / Alan Ockwell place second overall.

Leon Styles / Lisa Klassen demonstrate sideways style.

The competition would lie between Gubelmann and Yoon who would share the number of fastest times. Hoeck and Cavett were always following close behind.

When the teams pulled into Little Creek Casino at the finish, it was Gubelmann / Krolikowski who had won over Kosmides / Ockwell with Cavett / Secor in third.

Class wins went to Davis / Brandt for Open Two-Wheel and Kristopher Marciniak / Christine Wittish in their Dodge Neon took the Stock class.

In the championship standings, his fourth place put Hoeck into the top position with forty points— one ahead of Georgakopoulos, then Pastrana and Lawless.

Doug Heredos / Gabe West run through Nahwatzel in their Mazda.

Gary Cavett / Jeff Secor bring their Subaru into third place.

Wyeth Gubelmann has no plans to land nose first!

Olympus Rally - Schedule

Stage #	First Car	Stage Name	Miles
Saturday, May 20			
	10:00	Rally Start - Olympia	
1	10:35	Summit Loop 1	7.82
2	11:03	Maxwell Loop 1	5.07
3	11:26	Grays Harbor ORV Park 1	1.00
		Service - ORV Park	
4	12:39	Summit Loop 2	7.82
5	13:07	Maxwell Loop 2	5.07
6	13:30	Grays Harbor ORV Park 2	1.00
		Service - ORV Park	
7	15:13	Wildcat 1	12.93
8	15:56	Skookum 1	6.55
		Service - ORV Park	
9	17:59	Wildcat 2	12.93
10	18:42	Skookum 2	6.55
Sunday, May 21			
11	10:50	Stillwater 1	6.40
12	11:18	Cougar Meadow 1	6.52
13	11:46	Nahwatzel 1	19.76
		Service - Mill 5	
14	13:49	Stillwater 2	6.40
15	14:17	Cougar Meadow 2	6.52
16	14:45	Nahwatzel 2	19.76
	16:18	Rally Finish - Little Creek	

Above: Jamie Thomas / Matt Gauger approach the spectators at the Summit.

Below: Nathalie Richard co-drives for Blake Yoon.

Olympus Rally - Results

POSITION O'all	Cl	Class	Car #	Driver	Co-Driver	Car	Total
1	1	O4	103	Wyeth Gubelmann	Cindy Krolikowski	Subaru WRX STi	151:36:00
2	2	O4	22	Ralph Kosmides	Alan Ockwell	Subaru Impreza	154:27:00
3	3	O4	288	Gary Cavett	Jeff Secor	Subaru Impreza	155:51:00
4	4	O4	89	Wolfgang Hoeck	Piers O'Hanlon	Mitsubishi Lancer Evo 7	162:20:00
5	1	O2	60	Bruce Davis	Jimmy Brandt	Dodge Neon SRT-4	170:05:00
6	5	O4	376	Blake Yoon	Nathalie Richard	Mitsubishi Lancer Evo 7	174:59:00
7	1	S	761	Kristopher Marciniak	Christine Wittish	Dodge Neon	183:01:00
		S	258	Kris Dahl	Ed Dahl	Acura Integra GSR	DNF
		O4	211	Gabe vonAhlefeld	Jody Olson	Subaru Legacy	DNF
		O4	88	George Georgakopoulos	Faruq Mays	Subaru Impreza	DNF
		O4	207	Dave Hintz	Rick Hintz	Subaru WRX	DNF

Regional Event Entrants

SS	215	Jamie Thomas	Matt Gauger	Subaru WRX Wagon		
O4	233	Paul Eklund	Jeff Price	Subaru WRX		
PGT	285	Mike Goodwin	Debbie Wenzara	Subaru Impreza WRX		
O4	424	Mark Mager	Miller Dumaoal	Subaru Legacy		
H	374	Leon Styles	Lisa Klassen	Ford Escort Mk2		
O4	294	Barrett Dash	Tina Warner	Subaru STI		
O4	297	Steve Greer	Kelly Greer	Subaru Impreza		
P	232	Mark Tabor	Ben Bradley	Acura RSX		
G2	247	Chip Miller	Kathryn Hansen	Honda Civic		
PGT	271	Matt Tabor	Zeff Zurschmeide	Mazda 323 GTX		
G5	203	Doug Heredos	Gabe West	Mazda RX-7		
PGT	457	Ryan Barker	Kevin Laase	Subaru Impreza		
G2	240	Chris Blakely	Ian Pinter	VW GTI		
G5	269	John McKean	April Smith	Conquest		
H	439	Garth Ankeny	Russ Kraushaar	Saab 96		
P	132	Bruce Tabor	Tim Maple	Geo Metro		
O4	438	Victor Bartosek	DJ Flagg	Audi Quattro		
G2	404	Alex Needham	Bryce Reinhardt	Nissan Sentra		
P	231	Kristen Tabor	Janice Tabor	Nissan Sentra		
P	251	Lou Beck	Randee Hahn	Toyota MR2		
G5	459	Pat Harris	Eric Schild	Datsun 210		
G2	298	Jim Thomson	Rick Blackburn	VW GTI		
P	899	Scott Molvar	Chris Beebe	Nissan Sentra		
O4	205	Todd Lengacher	Merilee Joy Gilley	Audi S-1r		
P	649	Cody Crane	Brandon Buck	Honda CRX		

Above: Mark Tabor / Ben Bradley led the Tabor family challenge.

Below: Dave Hintz / Rick Hintz raise the dust.

Winners celebrate!

*Garth Ankeny / Russ
Kraushaar in their
beautfiully prepared Saab.*

*Mike Goodwin / Debbie Wenzara
jump at the ORV Park.*

Susquehannock Trail Performance Rally
Wellsboro, Pennsylvania
June 3, 2006

An excellent entry came out for the one-day endurance run—STPR—the fourth round of the Rally America Championship.

Mitsubishi teams were first in start order with Frank Sprongl / Daniel Sprongl being followed by Seamus Burke / Chrissie Beavis; Subaru had its regular rally teams of Travis Pastrana / Christian Edstrom and Ken Block / Alex Gelsomino; and Hyundai was represented by Antoine L'Estage / Mark Williams. Overseas visitors included Andrew Pinker / Robbie Durant (Australia) and Alfredo de Dominicis / Massimo Daddoveri (Italy). Lauchlin O'Sullivan / Scott Putnam and Matt Iorio / Ole Holter were leading the "private" Subaru entrants.

With an entry of more than sixty, there were a variety of cars, including a Datsun 280Z entered by Gregory Healey / John Macleod and a Mazda RX7 for Andrew Havas / John Dillon.

The route would use the regular roads of the Susquehannock and Tioga State forests. But the organizers had shaken up the itinerary, moving the Subaru Splash stage to be in the early afternoon. Unfortunately the rains in the weeks before

Matt Iorio / Ole Holter win STPR.

Left: Otis Dimiters / Alan Ockwell are first in Group N.

Mark McElduff / David Dooley go through the flying finish.

Gregory Healey / John Macleod run a Datsun 280Z in the regional events.

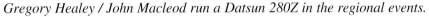

the event had caused the rivers to rise and in the end, the stage had to be canceled due to worries that cars could have been washed away by the flow.

First stage of the day was Asaph. It was taken by Pastrana five seconds ahead of L'Estage and Pinker sharing second place. Iorio came in fourth. Block lost time when he spun at the spectator area and had to be pushed to get started again—putting him out of contention. Later teams had to take a bogie time when the stage was canceled due to an on-stage crash.

Two more stages, Wilson Hollow and Thompson Hollows, would be run before lunch. Both stages were won by Block with no clear pattern behind him. At lunch the order was Pastrana, Iorio, O'Sullivan, Burke. With the tight racing, there were still six teams within thirty seconds of the leaders.

With the cancellation of Subaru Splash, the teams had a long layover before starting out for the evening session. There would be three stages run twice: Lee Stock, Lee Buck Francis and Lebo Mile are all challenging stages providing almost 100 miles of stage competition.

It was Iorio who settled in and took control. He won all three stages on the first pass through. His good times put him out in front—eleven seconds ahead of Pastrana then O'Sullivan.

Block's car had been running off the pace but he had the problem solved in time for stage 7 only to roll it onto its roof. He and Gelsomino were fine, but the team was out of the event. De Dominicis also had to retire due to mechanical problems.

On the second pass Pastrana was starting to catch Iorio until two punctures on stage 9 put him

Heavy rain causes mud pools to form on the stages. . . . Some teams took the opportunity to involve nearby spectators . . . .
Shown are the cars of Cook / Rhodes, Thompson / Dewey and Sorensen / Iden.

Travis Pastrana / Christian Edstrom would come in second.

John Dillon plans his strategy for the event.

The Pinker team at technical inspection.

out of contention. The stage also ended the run for Burke who rolled without injury. Stage wins went to Pastrana and O'Sullivan. Then Iorio came back to win the final stage and the event.

Despite having to run stage 10 with a flat tire, Pastrana / Edstrom came in second with O'Sullivan / Putnam third. Group 5 was won by Doug Shepherd / Pete Gladysz (Dodge SRT4); Group N by Otis Dimiters / Alan Ockwell (Subaru); Production GT by Matthew Johnson / Kim DeMotte (Subaru); Group 2 by Jon Nichols / Carl Schenk (VW GTI) and Production by Kenny Bartram / Dennis Hotson (VW Beetle).

After four rounds, the championship lead was being shared by Pastrana and Pinker, who both had fifty-two points. Block held third place then de Dominicis—neither having scored points at STPR.

Andrew Havas / John Dillon are second in Group 5.

Susquehannock Trail Performance Rally - Schedule

Stage #	First Car	Stage Name	Miles
Saturday, June 3			
	10:31	Rally Start - Wellsboro	
1	11:13	Asaph	10.03
2	12:05	Wilson Hollow	10.83
3	12:37	Thompson Hollows	8.99
		Service - Airport	
4	14:00	Subaru Splash	6.05
		Service - Airport	
5	17:31	Lee Stock 1	21.28
6	18:10	Lee Buck Francis 1	15.50
7	18:50	Lebo Mile 1	10.30
		Service - Germania	
8	21:07	Lee Stock 2	21.28
9	21:44	Lee Buck Francis 2	15.50
10	22:27	Lebo Mile 2	10.30
		Rally Finish - Wellsboro Airport	

Andrew Comrie-Picard / Marc Goldfarb would retire.

Allen Downs / Bernhardt Obry make a one-wheel landing.

Lauchlin O'Sullivan / Scott Putnam land hard on their way to third place.

David Anton / Dominik Joswiak cut the corner at night.

Susquehannock Trail Performance Rally - Results

POSITION O'all	POSITION Class	Class	Car #	Driver	Co-Driver	Car	Total
1	1	O	18	Matthew Iorio	Ole Holter	Subaru Impreza	1:44:13
2	2	O	199	Travis Pastrana	Christian Edstrom	Subaru Impreza WRX	1:45:03
3	3	O	90	Lauchlin O'Sullivan	Scott Putnam	Subaru WRX STi	1:45:07
4	4	O	606	Andrew Pinker	Robbie Durant	Subaru Impreza STi	1:46:51
5	5	O	19	Antoine L'Estage	Mark Williams	Hyundai Tiburon	1:47:01
6	6	O	116	Tom Lawless	Brian Sharkey	Mitsubishi Evo VIII	1:49:09
7	7	O	103	Wyeth Gubelmann	Cindy Krolikowski	Subaru Impreza WRX	1:52:17
8	1	G5	52	Doug Shepherd	Pete Gladysz	Dodge SRT4	1:52:17
9	1	GN	774	Otis Dimiters	Alan Ockwell	Subaru WRX STi	1:52:41
10	8	O	27	Chris Gilligan	Joe Petersen	Mitsubishi Evo IV	1:52:57
11	1	PGT	46	Matthew Johnson	Kim DeMotte	Subaru WRX	1:54:00
12	2	PGT	153	Eric Langbein	Jeremy Wimpey	Subaru WRX	1:54:38
13	3	PGT	429	Tanner Foust	Scott Crouch	Subaru Subaru WRX	1:54:56
14	2	G5	188	Andrew Havas	John Dillon	Mazda RX7	1:55:21
15	1	G2	97	Jon Nichols	Carl Schenk	Volkswagen GTI	1:56:08
16	9	O	145	Andy Brown	Alan Perry	Subaru STI	1:56:24
17	2	GN	100	David Anton	Dominick Joswiak	Subaru WRX STi	1:57:15
18	3	GN	945	Brendan Kelly	Keith Boyd	Subaru WRX	1:57:33
19	3	G5	26	Cary Kendall	Scott Friberg	Dodge SRT-4	1:58:55
20	4	G5	42	Eric Burmeister	Dave Shindle	Mazda Mazda 3	1:59:03
21	10	O	37	Chris Rhodes	Alexander Kihurani	Subaru STi	1:59:11
22	4	PGT	93	Robert Olson	Jason Takkunen	Subaru SRX	2:00:08
23	2	G2	70	Chris Duplessis	Edward McNelly	Volkswagen GTI	2:01:35
24	11	O	14	Amy BeberVanzo	Jeffrey Burmeister	Mitsubishi Evo VIII	2:02:13
25	5	G5	72	Jon Hamilton	Ken Sabo	Volkswagen TDI	2:02:49
26	12	O	705	Arthur Odero-Jowi	Jimmy Brandt	Eagle Talon	2:06:27
27	1	P	86	Kenny Bartram	Dennis Hotson	Volkswagen Beetle	2:07:51
28	13	O	102	George Georgakopoulos	Faruq Mays	Subaru Impreza WRS	2:08:53
29	5	PGT	133	Tom Young	Jim LeBeau	Subaru WRX	2:15:17
		O	25	Seamus Burke	Christine Beavis	Mitsubishi Evo 8	DNF
		O	20	Andrew Comrie-Picard	Marc Goldfarb	Mitsubishi Evo	DNF
		O	61	Frank Sprongl	Daniel Sprongl	Mitsubishi Evo VI	DNF
		O	77	Alfredo De Dominicis	Massimo Daddoveri	Mitsubishi Evo VII	DNF
		PGT	884	Timothy Stevens	Chris Stark	Subaru Impreza WRX	DNF
		PGT	59	Patrick Moro	Mike Rossey	Subaru WRX	DNF
		O	987	Peter Reilly	Ray Felice	Volkswagen Rally Golf	DNF
		O	43	Ken Block	Alessandro Gelsomino	Subaru Impreza WRX	DNF
		O	57	Dmitri Kishkarev	Alexander Korovkine	Mitsubishi Lancer Evo	DNF
		G2	47	Robin Jones	William Sekella	Volkswagen Golf	DNF
		G2	169	Eric Duncan	Matt Duncan	Honda Civic	DNF
		G2	111	Charles Kothe	Jeffrey Shu	Toyota Starlet	DNF
		PGT	66	Edward Mendham	Lise Mendham	Subaru WRX	DNF
		GN	91	Jonathan Bottoms	Carolyn Bosley	Subaru SRX STi	DNF
		O	10	Mark McElduff	David Dooley	Subaru WRX STi	DNF
		G5	15	Marcin Kowalski	Maciej Sawicki	Mitsubishi Eclipse	DNF

Regional Event Entrants

			907	Patrick Brennan	Sean Moriarty	Subaru WRX STi	
			874	Daniel O'Brien	Marc McAllister	Subaru Impreza STi	
			168	Celcus Donnelly	Martin Brady	Mitsubishi Evo VIII	
			878	Allen Downs Jr	Bernhard Obry	Subaru Impreza	
			779	Maciej Przybysz	Constantine Mantopoulos	Subaru Impreza	
			903	Christopher Sanborn	Donald DeRose	Ford Escort	
			572	James Robinson	Andrew Jessup	Acura RSX	
			763	Scott Wilburn	Carrie Wilburn	Subaru Impreza	
			601	Jon Miller	Scott Rhoades	Honda Prelude	
			280	Gregory Healey	John Macleod	Datsun 280Z	
			510	Daniel Cook	William Rhodes	Datsun 510	
			699	Luke Sorenson	John Iden	Saab 99	
			790	Larry Duane	Eamonn Sweeney	Toyota Corolla	
			848	Kathy Jarvis	Martin Headland	Volkswagen Golf	
			747	Brian Rutledge	Declan Brady	Subaru Impreza	
			631	Michael O'Leary	John O'Leary	Mitsubishi Evo 4	
			689	Tom McCabe	Brandon Ballos	Nissan Sentra	
			948	Chris Thompson	Steve Dewey	Honda Civic SI	
			480	Michael Gagnon	Karen Wagner	Ford Focus ZX3	
			44	David Furey	Noel Gallagher	Volkswagen GTI	
			931	Donald Kennedy	Matthew Kennedy	Subaru Impreza	
			755	Eoin McGeough	Bernard Farrell	Mitsubishi Evo	
			523	Travis Hanson	Terrance Hanson	Toyota Celica	
			622	Larry Parker	Bill Westrick	Mitsubishi VR4	
			15	Marcin Kowalski	Maciej Sawicki	Mitsubishi Eclipse	

Doug Shepherd / Pete Gladysz lift a wheel on their way to first in Group 5.

Not everyone needs 200 bhp to get around the event.

Alfredo de Dominicis / Massimo Daddoveri in their OSLV Mitsubishi.

Ole Holter and Matt Iorio relax after their first national victory.

Maine Forest Rally
Bethel, Maine
July 20–21, 2006

Above: Ramana Lagemann / Michael Fennell win Maine.

Left: Matt Iorio / Ole Holter win the spectator vote with their height.

The Maine Forest attracted a star-studded entry of sixty teams to compete on the fast and flowing forest roads at full speed.

The entry would be led by Paul Choiniere / Jeff Becker in their Hyundai Tiburon then the Subarus of Matt Iorio / Ole Holter, Ken Block / Alex Gelsomino and Travis Pastrana / Christian Edstrom. Mitsubishi entrants were led by Seamus Burke / Chrissie Beavis and Alfredo de Dominicis (Dedo) / Massimo Daddoveri.

Road availability was an issue as many of the region's forests had changed ownership and the traditional stage roads were no longer available. As usual, the event would start at the Mexico Recreation Area with a Parc Exposé and Super Special stage. Then the teams would head north to Oquossoc for two runnings of the South Arm stage before returning to Mexico for the high-speed jumps of Concord Pond.

On Saturday the teams would start heading west to tackle the rough roads of Dillon-Success twice before heading to the north again to Oquossoc for Middle Dam (In and Out).

The weather held and was warm—if not hot—throughout the event, although a shower before the start of the event held the dust in place.

The organizers had added a jump to the Super Special stage in Mexico Rec. They started with a parade lap of the stage. For the benefit of the spectators the teams were allowed to take the jump at speed and most did just that. Some found the jump so challenging, and damaging, that when it came to the actual stage they dialed back the power and were happy to get through without further damage. The exception was Iorio, who instantly became the crowd favorite when he seemed to clear even more height the second time through. The stage went to Pastrana but, with only half a mile in

Above: Paul Choiniere / Jeff Becker would retire on the first day.

Below: Tim Penasack / Nathalie Richard plow the road on landing.

Kenny Bartram prepares the car at Parc Exposé.

Chrissie Beavis prepares for the event.

Daniel Cook / William Rhodes would win Group 2.

The helmets of Amy Bebervanzo / Alex Kihurani.

Tanner Foust / Scott Crouch raise a dust trail.

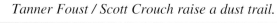

length, his lead was minimal—with five teams sharing second place one second behind him.

Antoine L'Estage / Mark Williams set the day's pace taking all three stages after the Super Special. On both passes of South Arm it was Block who was challenging L'Estage with Dedo and Choiniere close behind.

In the dusk at Concord Pond, second fastest went to Choiniere, followed by Andrew Comrie-Picard (ACP) / Marc Goldfarb. Block dropped out of contention when he lost ten minutes after he ripped a wheel off on a tree. He limped out of the stage and the Vermont SportsCar team was able to effect repairs so he could continue the second day.

At the end of the first day, with twenty-six stage miles behind them, L'Estage led Choiniere from ACP and Dedo.

Day two started with Dedo showing his speed, taking stage 5 ahead of ACP and Ramana Lagemann / Michael Fennell. The organizers had planned to run a short stage 6, Mountain Top, inside the Dillon-Success area. But it was decided to be too rough for even this tough event. So the teams immediately returned along Success-Dillon. Once again it was Dedo who won, this time from Iorio and Lagemann. The roads were rough enough to unlock the hood on the Mitsubishi of ACP. It flew open damaging the windscreen. The team lost time as they continued to the end of the stage before they could secure the hood again.

Above: Vittorio Bares / Susanna Bares tackle Dillon-Success in their Audi.

Richard Duplessis / Ed McNelly compete in the regional event.

Maine Forest Rally - Schedule

Stage #	First Car	Stage Name	Miles
Friday - July 20			
	4:10	Rally Start	
1	14:51	Mexico Rec	0.5
2	15:44	South Arm South	9.9
3	17:20	South Arm North	9.9
		Service	
4	19:34	Concord Pond	5.6
Saturday - July 21			
5	9:54	Dillon-Success	12.7
6	10:19	Mountain Top	3.6
7	11:25	Success-Dillon	12.7
		Service	
8	14:13	Middle Dam In	13.7
9	15:40	Middle Dam Out	15.3
	17:33	Rally Finish - Sunday River	

Above: Jonathan Bottoms / Carolyn Bosley win Group N.

The stage also cost L'Estage his lead when he lost twenty seconds misreading the junction at the spectator area. Then on Middle Dam he would have to retire due to mechanical failure.

The last two stages were taken by ACP from Lagemann on the way in and Pastrana on the way out. Despite ACP's fast times, it was Dedo who was leading as the cars arrived at the finish, but he was found to have been late in arriving at the second day Parc Exposé and was given a twenty-four second penalty—dropping him from first overall to fifth.

Showing how important a steady drive is at this tough event, the win went to Lagemann / Fennell from Pastrana / Edstrom with Iorio / Holter in third.

Matthew Johnson is interviewed for TV.

Above: Larry Duane / Eamonn Sweeney in their Toyota Corolla.

Below: Antoine L'Estage / Mark Williams almost miss the turn.

Maine Forest Rally - Results

POSITION O'All	Class	Class	Car #	Driver	Co-Driver	Car	Total
1	1	O	74	Ramana Lagemann	Michael Fennell	Ford Escort	1:06:08.7
2	2	O	199	Travis Pastrana	Christian Edstrom	Subaru WRX Sti	1:06:15.5
3	3	O	18	Matthew Iorio	Ole Holter	Subaru Impreza	1:06:17.6
4	4	O	20	Andrew Comrie-Picard	Marc Goldfarb	Mitsubishi Evo 4	1:06:17.7
5	5	O	77	Alfredo DeDominicis	Massimo Daddoveri	Mitsubishi Evo 8	1:06:21.4
6	6	O	116	Thomas Lawless	Rod Hendricksen	Mitsubishi Evo 8	1:07:37.0
7	1	PGT	429	Tanner Foust	Scott Crouch	Subaru WRX	1:08:33.3
8	7	O	30	George Plsek	Jeffrey Burmeister	Mitsubishi Evo	1:09:18.1
9	1	GN	91	Jonathan Bottoms	Carolyn Bosley	Subaru WRX STI	1:13:31.7
10	8	O	110	John Cassidy	Erik Lee	Subaru WRX	1:14:22.2
11	9	O	102	George Georgakopoulos	Faruq Mays	Subaru WRX	1:15:23.1
12	10	O	453	Jean-Louis Weid	Freddy Weil	Subaru Impreza	1:15:47.2
13	11	O	43	Ken Block	Alessandro Gelsomino	Subaru STi	1:16:05.1
14	12	O	690	Kenny Bartram	Dennis Hotson	Subaru WRX	1:17:06.3
15	13	O	14	Amy BeberVanzo	Alexander Kihurani	Mitsubishi Evo 8	1:17:09.0
16	2	PGT	66	Edward Mendham	Lise Mendham	Subaru WRX	1:17:16.3
17	1	G2	510	Daniel Cook	William Rhodes	Datsun 510	1:19:25.3
18	2	G2	47	Robin Jones	William Sekella	VW Golf	1:19:27.1
19	14	O	631	Michael O'Leary	John O'Leary	Mitsubishi Evo 4	1:21:21.0
20	1	G5	60	Bruce Davis	Jimmy Brandt	Dodge Neon SRT4	1:23:22.0
21	3	PGT	46	Matthew Johnson	Kim DeMotte	Subaru WRX	1:25:56.1
22	1	P	848	Kathy Jarvis	Martin Headland	VW GTI	1:28:11.4
23	3	G2	862	Dan Brosnan	Jeffrey Hagan	Nissan Sentra	1:29:20.1
24	2	GN	100	David Anton	Dominik Jozwiak	Subaru WRX STi	1:30:07.4
25	4	PGT	523	Travis Hanson	Terrance Hanson	Subaru WRX	1:30:53.4
26	2	P	797	John Arango	William Doyle	BMW 325i	1:41:29.9
27	5	PGT	93	Robert Olson	Ryan Johnson	Subaru WRX	1:52:16.0
		O	874	Daniel O'Brien	Jeremy Wimpey	Subaru STi	DNF
		G2	70	Chris Duplessis	Edward McNelly	VW GTI	DNF
		GN	151	Josh Chang	Jeff Cruzan	Subaru WRX	DNF
		O	17	Antoine L'Estage	Mark Williams	Hyundai Tiburon	DNF
		PGT	59	Patrick Moro	Mike Rossey	Subaru WRX	DNF
		O	10	Mark McElduff	Eddie Fries		DNF
		O	173	Patrick Lilly	Noel Gallagher	Subaru WRX	DNF
		PGT	19	Timothy Penasack	Nathalie Richard	Subaru WRX	DNF
		O	11	Paul Choiniere	Jeff Becker	Hyundai Tiburon	DNF
		O	25	Seamus Burke	Christine Beavis	Mitsubishi Evo 8	DNF
		O	103	Wyeth Gubelmann	Cynthia Krolikowski	Subaru Impreza	DNF
		O	774	Otis Dimiters	Alan Ockwell	Subaru Impreza	DNF
		G5	42	Eric Burmeister	Dave Shindle	Mazda 3	DNF

Regional Event Entrants

874	Daniel O'Brien	Jeremy Wimpey	Subaru STi
69	Charles Sherrill	Joshua Bressem	Mitsubishi Evo 4
878	Allen Downs Jr	Bernhard Obry	Subaru Impreza
779	Maciej Przybysz	Robert Amato	Subaru Impreza
523	Travis Hanson	Terrance Hanson	Subaru WRX
763	Scott Wilburn	Carrie Wilburn	Subaru Impreza
510	Daniel Cook	William Rhodes	Datsun 510
778	Dave Getchell	Steve McKelvie	Subaru 2.5RS
548	Matt Bushore	Andrew Bushore	VW Jetta
630	Vittorio Bares	Suzanna Bares	Audi 4000
631	Michael O'Leary	John O'Leary	Mitsubishi Evo 4
747	Brian Rutledge	Bernard Farrell	Subaru Impreza RS
790	Larry Duane	Eamonn Sweeney	Toyota Corolla
910	Martin Egan	Thomas Byrne	Toyota Corolla
299	Jason Hynd	Timothy Hynd	Eagle Talon
762	Sean Sosik-Hamor	Andrew Hobgood	Subaru Impreza
797	John Arango	William Doyle	BMW 325i
848	Kathy Jarvis	Martin Headland	VW GTI
862	Dan Brosnan	Jeffrey Hagan	Nissan Sentra
304	David Furey	Damien Treanor	VW GTI
907	Patrick Brennan	Stephen Duffy	Subaru STi
984	Joao Ferreira	Niall Johnson	VW GTI

Class wins went to Tanner Foust / Scott Crouch in PGT, Jonathan Bottoms / Carolyn Bosley in Group N, Daniel Cook / William Rhodes in Group 2, Bruce Davis / Jimmy Brandt in Group 5, and Kathy Jarvis / Martin Headland in Production.

In the race for the title, his steady drive had given Pastrana a seventeen-point lead ahead joint second-place drivers Andrew Pinker and Ken Block.

Ken Block / Alex Gelsomino entertain the crowds at the Spectator Stage.

Ken Block is interviewed at Parc Exposé.

Tim Penasack / Nathalie Richard on the night stages.

Ojibwe Forests Rally
Bemidji, Minnesota
August 25–26, 2006

Travis Pastrana / Christian Edstrom get their first Rally America win.

Left: Mike Hurst / Russell Norton run through the open countryside.

Teams arrived in Bemidji for the Ojibwe Forests Rally with Travis Pastrana, co-driven by Christian Edstrom, holding a seventeen-point lead in the driver's championship. In joint second place were teammate Ken Block, and Andrew Pinker. Block had entered with regular co-driver Alex Gelsomino, but Pinker was not competing this time.

Other Open Class entries came from Alfredo de Dominicis (Dedo) / Massimo Daddoveri and Matt Iorio / Ole Holter. Leading the PGT entries were Tanner Foust / Chrissie Beavis and Matthew Johnson / Kim DeMotte

The action would start in the early evening of Friday with a Super Special stage held at the Bemidji Speedway. The teams would then spend the rest of Friday evening in Paul Bunyan State Forest covering fifty-five stage miles. Saturday's daylight stages were centered in Itasca State Park and would add another seventy-two miles to the stage count.

The Super Special stage was taken by Otis Dimiters with co-driver Alan Ockwell with a time of 53.7 seconds. Behind them, and all within three seconds, came Block, Dedo and Pastrana.

Otis Dimiters / Alan Ockwell would retire early.

It was Block who took the first forest stage (Halverson Lake) by three seconds over Pastrana and Dedo. But then three miles into the third stage he met a tree and center-punched the car. His event was over.

The stage was taken by Pastrana from Iorio and Dedo. Then Dedo took the fourth stage so that as the cars pulled into the first service, the four stages had been won by four teams.

Already, retirements included Sans Thompson / Craig Marr who had the engine blow in their newly rebuilt Dodge Neon and Dimiters who ran out of gas on stage 4.

The Friday night stages started with Akeley Cutoff, which was won by Pastrana from Iorio. Pastrana also took the next stage but Iorio came back to win the last two stages of the night from Pastrana, Dedo and Foust.

At the end of the first day, Pastrana was leading by a mere two seconds from Iorio, then Dedo, Foust and Johnson.

The second day turned out to be a one-sided battle between Pastrana and Iorio. There were a total of nine stages covering more than seventy miles. Pastrana took all but one of the stages, with Iorio taking one win and second on all the others. Behind them Dedo was holding a comfortable third place until he had to retire on stage 14. This promoted Foust to third, but he lost the podium position when he lost ten minutes on stage 16, allowing Johnson to come through to take third.

Carolyn Bosley and Jonathan Bottoms at the drivers' briefing

Matt Iorio / Ole Holter make second place.

Eric Burmeister / Dave Shindle at full speed at dusk.

Alfredo de Dominicis (R) and Massimo Daddoveri can take it easy at Parc Exposé . . .

. . . but are fully committed on stage.

After 128 miles of stages Pastrana / Edstrom won their first Rally America championship event and extended their lead in the championship race. Iorio / Holter came second and Johnson / DeMotte were third overall and took the PGT class. Other class wins went to David Anton / Dominik Jozwiak (Group N), Cary Kendall / Scott Friberg (Group 5), Kathy Jarvis / Martin Headland (Production).

Jonathan Bottoms / Carolyn Bosley jump into the arena.

Henry Krolikowski / Cindy Krolikowski kick up dust on Duck Lake.

Left: Mark Utecht / Rob Bohn would compete in the regional event.

*Matt Bushore / Karen Wagner
find a new way to finish the
stage.*

Ojibwe Forests Rally - Schedule

Stage #	First Car	Stage Name	Miles
Friday - August 25			
	7:00	Rally Start	
1	17:04	Bemidji Speedway	0.60
2	17:52	Halverson Lake	5.28
3	18:19	Refuge	13.17
4	18:55	Blue Trail	11.48
		Service - Akeley	
5	21:00	Akeley Cutoff	9.46
6	21:29	Spur 1	13.76
7	21:50	Spur 2	25.17
8	22:13	Kabekona	6.60
Saturday - August 26			
9	14:07	Heart Lake	7.21
10	14:38	Walde Trail	2.44
11	15:01	Little Rock	7.34
12	15:38	Moulton Lake	6.93
13	16:10	Indian Creek	9.50
		Service - Osage	
14	18:30	Duck Lake	9.50
15	19:07	Basswood Lake	3.96
16	19:47	Strawberry Mountain	22.54
17	20:40	Otterkill	3.00
	21:50	Rally Finish	

*Mark Larson
briefs the teams.*

Erick Nelson / Greg Messler win Group 5 on one of the regionals.

Ojibwe Forests Rally - Results

O'all	Class	Class	Car #	Driver	Co-Driver	Car	Total
1	1	O	199	Travis Pastrana	Christian Edstrom	Subaru Impreza WRX STi	2:06:47.9
2	2	O	18	Matthew Iorio	Ole Holter	Subaru Impreza	2:08:02.3
3	1	PGT	46	Matthew Johnson	Kim DeMotte	Subaru WRX	2:15:40.2
4	3	O	27	Chris Gilligan	Joe Petersen	Mitsubishi Evo IV	2:16:06.4
5	1	GN	100	David Anton	Dominik Jozwiak	Subaru WRX STi	2:17:24.4
6	4	O	44	Henry Krolikowski	Cindy Krolikowski	Subaru Impreza	2:18:56.9
7	2	PGT	153	Eric Langbein	Jeremy Wimpey	Subaru WRX	2:20:24.3
8	3	PGT	84	Greg Drozd	John Nordlie	Subaru Impreza	2:24:29.5
9	5	O	207	Dave Hintz	Rick Hintz	Subaru WRX	2:27:32.5
10	2	GN	91	Jonathan Bottoms	Carolyn Bosley	Subaru WRX STi	2:28:20.3
11	4	PGT	429	Tanner Foust	Christine Beavis	Subaru WRX	2:30:36.7
12	5	PGT	67	Bryan Pepp	Jerry Stang	Subaru WRX	2:31:34.0
13	6	O	510	Mike Hurst	Russell Norton	Subaru STi	2:35:04.2
14	1	G5	26	Cary Kendall	Scott Friberg	Dodge SRT-4	2:36:07.1
15	2	G5	92	Paul Dunn	Bill Westrick	Dodge Neon SRT4	2:38:21.5
16	1	P	113	Kathy Jarvis	Martin Headland	VW Golf	2:42:45.4
17	3	G5	60	Bruce Davis	Jimmy Brandt	Dodge Neon SRT-4	2:43:45.6
		O	77	Alfredo DeDominicis	Massimo Daddoveri	Mitsubishi Evo	DNF
		O	93	Bob Olson	Ryan Johnson	Subaru Impreza	DNF
		G5	42	Eric Burmeister	Dave Shindle	Mazda 3	DNF
		O	774	Otis Dimiters	Alan Ockwell	Subaru Impeza	DNF
		G2	49	Sans Thompson	Craig Marr	Dodge Neon ACR	DNF
		G2	169	Eric Duncan	Matt Duncan	Honda Civic DX	DNF
		O	43	Ken Block	Alessandro Gelsomino	Subaru Impreza WRX STi	DNF

Regional Event Entrants

64	Robert Borowicz	Mariusz Borowicz	Subaru Impreza WRX Sti
83	Mark Utecht	Rob Bohn	Ford Mustang
550	Kyle Sarasin	Stuart Sarasin	Mitsubishi Eclipse
207	Dave Hintz	Rick Hintz	Subaru WRX
413	Erik Schmidt	Michael Rose	Subaru Impreza
548	Matt Bushore	Karen Wagner	Volkswagen Jetta
570	Erik Payeur	Adam Payeur	Mitsubishi Galant
486	Martin Menning	Ryan Schnell	Subaru Impreza
744	Paul Koll	Matthew Wappler	VW Golf GTi
562	Scott Justus	Dave Parps	Nissan Sentra SER
558	James Cox	Chris Stark	Chevrolet SL2
433	Mitchell Williams	Alix Hakala	Subaru Impreza
527	Jonah Liubakka	Craig Walli	Saturn SL2
403	Erick Nelson	Greg Messler	Plymouth Laser
319	Chris Greenhouse	Donald DeRose	Plymouth Neon
686	Heath Nunnemacher	Travis Hanson	Subaru WRX
515	Adam Boullion	Philip Boullion	Ford Focus
591	David Cizmas	Jacob Himes	Mazda RX-7
628	Dan Adamson	Jeremiah Schubitzke	Saturn SL
696	Bryan Holder	Tracy Payeur	Saturn SL2
687	Chad Eixenberger	Jay Luikart	VW Golf

Winners celebrate.

Guess who?

Below: Greg Drozd / John Nordlie on Duck Lake.

Below: Matt Johnson / Kim DeMotte on their way to a class win and third overall.

International Rally Tennessee

Linden, Tennessee
September 2–3, 2006

Seamus Burke / Chrissie Beavis win the event.

Left: Josh Wimpey / Jeremy Wimpey win the Modified 2 class.

Perry County hosted a round of the U.S. Rally Championship for the first time in September. The event would use the sinuous roads around Linden to offer an all-asphalt event.

Each day of the two days of competition the teams would follow the same basic format. The mornings would be spent to the northwest of the town—with the stages bumping up against the Tennessee River. Then in the afternoons the core of the event would be the Old Hohenwald-Linden road twisting its way along the Sassafras Stand Ridge.

The top of the entry list was dominated by Mitsubishi teams including last year's winner Celsus Donnelly with co-driver Noel Gallagher, Seamus Burke with Chrissie Beavis and championship leader Wolfgang Hoeck with Piers O'Hanlon. Daniel O'Brien / Dominik Jozwiak and Brian Scott / John Dillon would lead the Subaru entries. Two-wheel drive classes would have a good mix of entries, including Acuras, Volkswagens and Fords.

Andrew Frick / Simon Wright lift a wheel on Old Hohenwald.

Dave Carapetyan / Justin Kwak have a difficult weekend.

Robert Mannz / Mark Sackett raise a wheel on Old Linden.

The man to beat throughout the weekend would be Burke. On the first stage—Tree Farm—he took joint fastest time with O'Brien, followed by Donnelly and Scott;

then on Owl Hollow he would take an eleven-second lead over Scott followed by O'Brien. On the second run of Tree Farm, Donnelly would have to pull out with a blown clutch. The stage would be taken by Blake Yoon, co-driven by Alex Kihurani. The final stage of the morning would see Burke back at the top, this time with Hoeck behind him.

By lunchtime on Friday Burke had a seventeen-second lead over O'Brien then Yoon. The afternoon session would provide three runs along the Old Hohenwald stage. Burke took fastest time on each run with Yoon, O'Brien and Hoeck each taking second honors once. Yoon, though, would end his event prematurely when he left the road on stage 6. At the end of the day, Burke led the field by over a minute from O'Brien then Hoeck and Scott.

The second day provided an almost clean sweep for Burke as he took all but one of the stages—that being the second stage of the day, Strickland, which was won by Scott. Behind Burke, the fight among O'Brien, Hoeck and Scott would continue throughout the day. In the end, it was O'Brien / Jozwiak who came in second two and a half minutes behind Burke / Beavis but just twenty-six seconds ahead of Hoeck / O'Hanlon.

O'Brien would also take the Prototype 1 class win. Other class wins would go to Brian Rutledge / Amy Feistal (Super Stock), Josh Wimpey / Jeremy Wimpey (Modified 2), Bruce Davis / Jimmy Brandt (Open 2wd), Robert Mannz / Mark Sackett (Stock), John Barnett / Greg Marvin (Modified 1).

Gerard Coffey / Dave Dooley only lose ten seconds from this excursion.

Wolfgang Hoeck / Piers O'Hanlon on their way to third overall.

Lunchtime for Daniel O'Brien, Dominik Jozwiak, John Dillon, Brian Scott.

In the championship standings, Hoeck held his lead but with a reduced margin—having 71 points against Burke's 67. With two rounds left, it was all still to play for.

Daniel O'Brien / Dominik Jozwiak are second overall.

Darrell Pugh / Jonathan Barnes have to brake hard on Old Linden.

Rally Tennessee - Schedule

Stage #	First Car	Stage Name	Miles
Saturday - September 2			
	9:30	Rally Start	
1	9:41	Tree Farm 1	5.68
2	10:11	Owl Hollow 1	4.78
		Service	
3	11:47	Tree Farm 2	5.68
4	12:17	Owl Hollow 2	4.78
		Service	
5	13:32	Old Hohenwald 1	12.63
6	14:44	Old Hohenwald 2	12.63
		Service	
7	17:41	Old Hohenwald 3	12.63
Sunday - September 3			
8	10:26	Bunker Hill 1	4.78
9	10:55	Strickland 1	5.68
		Service	
10	13:00	Bunker Hill 2	4.78
11	13:29	Strickland 2	5.68
		Service	
12	14:43	Old Linden 1	12.66
13	15:35	Old Linden 2	12.66
		Service	
14	18:15	Old Linden 3	12.66

Above: Alex Kihurani and Faruq Mays swap stories while waiting for the start.

Bryn Walters / Sharon Walters in their Ford Focus.

*John Barnett / Greg Marvin
entertain on their way to
first in M1 class.*

Rally Tennessee - Results

POSITION O'all	Class	Class	Car #	Driver	Co-Driver	Car	Total
1	1	O4	2	Seamus Burke	Chrissie Beavis	Mitsubishi Evo VIII	1:37:38
2	1	P1	4	Daniel O'Brien	Dominik Jozwiak	Subaru WRX STi	1:40:15
3	2	O4	3	Wolfgang Hoeck	Piers O'Hanlon	Mitsubishi Evo	1:40:41
4	3	O4	7	Brian Scott	John Dillon	Subaru WRX STi	1:42:24
5	2	P1	6	Enda McCormack	Kieran McElhinney	Mitsubishi Evo VI	1:43:56
6	4	O4	10	Gerard Coffey	Dave Dooley	Mitsubishi Evo VIII	1:44:24
7	5	O4	12	George Georgakopoulos	Faruq Mays	Subaru WRX STi	1:44:32
8	3	P1	8	Darrell Pugh	Jonathan Barnes	Mitsubishi Eclipse	1:47:21
9	1	SS	16	Brian Rutledge	Amy Feistel	Subaru Impreza	1:47:39
10	1	M2	11	Josh Wimpey	Jeremy Wimpey	VW Golf GTi	1:49:39
11	1	O2	13	Bruce Davis	Jimmy Brandt	Dodge SRT-4	1:52:39
12	2	M2	17	Andrew Frick	Simon Wright	VW Scirocco	1:58:53
13	3	M2	18	Bryn Walters	Sharon Walters	Ford Focus ZX3	1:58:59
14	1	S	21	Robert Mannz	Mark Sackett	Ford Escort	2:04:16
15	1	M1	19	John Barnett	Greg Marvin	VW Scirocco	2:05:06
16	2	S	20	Ronald Vecchioni	Levi Magyar	Mazda RX-7	2:09:37
17	2	M1	15	Michael Hall	Dave Stockdill	Mitsubishi Mighty Max	
		O4	9	Blake Yoon	Alex Kihurani	Subaru WRX	
		O4	1	Celsus Donnelly	Noel Gallagher	Mitsubishi Evo VIII	
		P1	14	Jason Hynd	Jacob Rupert	Eagle Talon	
		O2	5	Dave Carapetyan	Justin Kwak	Acura Integra Type-R	
		M1	22	Dave Stockdill	Sarah Grenier	Mitsubishi Mighty Max	

*Noel Gallagher, Brian Rutledge (C) and Alisa Dean
relax at service.*

Seamus Burke relaxes after a hard day of driving.

Right: Enda McCormack / Kieran McElhinney kick up the dust.

Right: Daniel O'Brien and Otis Dimiters check out American Rally Action *(volume one!).*

Left: Brian Scott / John Dillon go cross-country.

Colorado Cog Rally
Steamboat Springs, Colorado
September 23–24, 2006

Left: David Anton / Dominik Jozwiak keep control and stay on the road.

Above: Travis Pastrana / Christian Edstrom on their way to another win.

The story of the 2006 Colorado Cog is the story of mud. The weather during the event itself was dry and fine but, in the days leading up to the start, there had been enough rain to make parts of the course treacherous. The last shower went through during the Parc Exposé—forcing the teams to take shelter along the edges of the buildings in downtown Steamboat Springs.

By the time the event started the next day, the showers had stopped but two of the stages had to be canceled—deemed impassable when some volunteers in four-wheel-drive SUVs got stuck. Most of the rest of the stages were fine but in some parts the underlying surface had dried enough that the remaining mud acted like ice—catching out the unwary competitor and sending them in a straight line wherever the laws of physics took them.

The route had been scheduled using the county roads mainly to the north of Hayden in the Routt National Forest.

The Subaru Rally Team USA had entered Travis Pastrana / Christian Edstrom and Ken

Nathan Conley / Brandye Monks end their event in the mud.

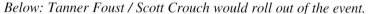

Below: Tanner Foust / Scott Crouch would roll out of the event.

Block / Alex Gelsomino—hoping to solidify their lead in the championship. Matt Iorio / Ole Holter and Brian Scott / John Dillon led the non-works Subarus, while the Mitsubishi challenge was led by Andrew Comrie-Picard (ACP) / Marc Goldfarb. The Italian team of Alfredo de Dominicis had entered, but the preparation of his car had not been completed and he had to withdraw.

In the PGT class, Matthew Johnson / Kim DeMotte and Tanner Foust / Scott Crouch would continue their season-long duel.

The event started with the Wolf Mountain stage taking the teams from Steamboat Springs towards Hayden and it was clear that Pastrana and Iorio were going to continue their dogfight from Ojibwe. Iorio took the honors from Pastrana followed by ACP and Block.

With Elkhead Loop (stages 2 and 4) canceled, it was Pastrana who took the first run through Middle Cog from Block and Iorio; then Block who won over Pastrana and ACP on the second run.

John Conley / Steven Treml in their Dodge Colt.

After the Super Special stage at the fairgrounds, the teams were able to service the cars and clear mud from the wheel wells. It was Pastrana leading from Block and Iorio.

The centerpiece of the afternoon would be two runs on the Stokes Gulch-Breeze Basin roads. Those who went to the mid-point spectator area were treated to some high-speed action as the teams fought with the mud. Many were caught out including Nathan Conley / Brandye Monks who slow-rolled their Subaru out of the event—fortunately without any injury.

On the first time through, Block took the stage from ACP and Pastrana but had to retire when his engine blew as he crossed the finish line. Without him, the competition became a fight between Pastrana and Iorio with ACP always close by. The teams then went north to race up Middle Cog before returning to Breeze Basin. Pastrana took Middle Cog then Iorio took the return visit to Breeze Basin and the final stage of the day—Flow Mountain.

Right: Matthew Johnson / Kim DeMotte are first in PGT class.

Below: Matt Iorio / Ole Holter are second overall.

At the end of the first day, Pastrana was leading Iorio by twenty-four seconds with ACP lying third, one minute behind. In the fight for PGT, Foust was leading Johnson by forty-three seconds.

The Saturday would include thirty-seven miles of competition over seven stages.

The conditions had improved with the roads having had twenty-four hours to dry, but there were still corners that would prove to be muddy and challenging. Pastrana started the day leading and held his position—taking five of the stages with Iorio and ACP taking one apiece.

As the teams arrived at the finish, Pastrana / Edstrom had won by a margin of forty-two seconds from Iorio / Holter with Comrie-Picard / Goldfarb third. Johnson / DeMotte took PGT when

Foust rolled out of the competition on the last stage. Other class winners were David Anton / Dominik Jozwiak (Group N), Kenny Bartram / Dennis Hotson (Production), John Conley / Steven Tremi (Group 5) and Eric Duncan / Matt Duncan (Group 2).

Colorado Cog Rally - Schedule

Stage #	First Car	Stage Name	Miles
Saturday - September 23			
	8:01	Rally Start	
1	8:53	Wolf Mountain	4.10
2	10:01	Elkhead Loop 1	8.20
3	10:27	Middle Cog 1	5.22
4	11:03	Elkhead Loop 2	8.20
5	11:29	Middle Cog 2	5.22
6	11:58	Fairgrounds 1	1.07
		Service	
7	13:37	Stokes Gulch	12.84
8	14:13	Middle Cog 3	6.85
		Service	
9	16:07	Breeze Basin	12.85
10	16:55	Flow Mountain	4.13
Sunday - September 24			
11	9:46	Sage Creek 1	5.86
12	10:34	Middle Cog 4	6.81
13	10:55	Elkhead Flats 1	6.22
14	11:35	Fairgrounds 2	1.07
		Service	
15	13:29	Sage Creek 2	5.85
16	14:11	Elkhead Flats 2	6.23
17	14:32	Middle Cog 5	5.22
	15:44	Rally Finish	

Christopher Moore / Bo Randolph climb from the start of Middle Cog.

Robert Olson / Ryan Johnson in the mud of the fairgrounds.

Above: Andrew Comrie-Picard / Marc Goldfarb place third overall.

Colorado Cog Rally - Results

POSITION O'all	POSITION Class	Class	Car #	Driver	Co-Driver	Car	TOTAL
1	1	O	199	Travis Pastrana	Christian Edstrom	Subaru Impreza WRX STi	1:23:34.8
2	2	O	18	Matthew Iorio	Ole Holter	Subaru Impreza	1:24:16.2
3	3	O	20	Andrew Comrie-Picard	Marc Goldfarb	Mitsubishi Evo IV	1:25:15.7
4	1	PGT	46	Matthew Johnson	Kim DeMotte	Subaru WRX	1:30:59.8
5	4	O	93	Robert Olson	Ryan Johnson	Subaru Impreza	1:31:52.4
6	1	GN	100	David Anton	Dominik Jozwiak	Subaru Impreza STi	1:32:02.1
7	5	O	96	Brian Scott	John Dillon	Subaru WRX STi	1:32:53.8
8	1	P	690	Kenny Bartram	Dennis Hotson	VW Beetle	1:49:52.9
9	1	G5	441	John Conley	Steven Tremi	Dodge Colt	1:55:39.2
10	1	G2	169	Eric Duncan	Matt Duncan	Honda Civic	1:59:21.5
11	2	P	113	Kathy Jarvis	Emily Burton-Weinman	VW Golf	2:14:27.8
		PGT	429	Tanner Foust	Scott Crouch	Subaru WRX	DNF
		O	421	Jason Waples	Rebecca Greek	Subaru WRX STi	DNF
		O	43	Ken Block	Alessandro Gelsomino	Subaru Impreza WRX STi	DNF
		PGT	710	Nathan Conley	Brandye Monks	Subaru WRX	DNF
		GN	24	Todd Moberly	Ray Moberly	Subaru STi	DNF

Regional Event Entrants

413	Erik Schmidt	Michael Rose	Subaru Impreza
449	Mark Malsom	Grant Hughes	Subaru Impreza
418	Jimmy Keeney	Melissa Salas	Honda Civic
436	Tommy Kilpatrick	Michael Kilpatrick	Honda Civic
486	Martin Menning	Ryan Schnell	Subaru Impreza
608	Christopher Moore	Bo Randolph	Dodge Colt
402	Fred Zietz	Devon Colson	Honda CRX

The crowd's favorite, though, had to be Kathy Jarvis / Emily Burton-Weinman who had struggled through the whole of the event. Their problems started with a failed water pump but the overheating caused the engine to misfire. They ran most of the stages on the second day on three cylinders—losing twenty-five minutes to class winner Bartram, but still managed to finish.

With two rounds of the Rally America Championship left, Pastrana would leave Steamboat Springs with a controlling lead of 113 points to Iorio on 76 and Block in third with 54.

Winners celebrate.

Above: Jason Waples, Ray Moberly,
Todd Moberly.

Above, right: Jason Waples / Rebecca Greek collect a fence post during one excursion.

Cars line up for the
start of Middle Cog.

Prescott Rally
Prescott, Arizona
October 6–7, 2006

With the U.S. Rally Championship reaching its climax, the main contenders went to the high desert of Arizona for the penultimate round. This was the first time that the Prescott Rally was included in the USRC. The event was kept compact with all the action taking place around Perkinsville to the northeast of Prescott. The stages would use the three roads that provide access to the town land in various combinations.

Wolfgang Hoeck, co-driven by Piers O'Hanlon, was leading the standings by a slim margin from Seamus Burke with Chrissie Beavis. Both teams were in Mitsubishis. Subaru teams included George Georgakopoulos / Faruq Mays and Brian Scott / John Dillon and both still had the points tally to be able to win the championship. Mike Whitman / Bill Westrick had their popular Ford Escort RS out to challenge the Mitsubishi and Subaru dominance while Leon Styles / Tracy Manspeaker had their much older Ford Escort out to demonstrate rear-wheel driving techniques.

Scrutineering and the practice stage were held

Above: Brian Scott / John Dillon jump on their way to second.

Left: Seamus Burke / Chrissie Beavis at the fairground.

"If I was allowed to drive, I could win!"

Left: Michael Taylor at the Tech inspection.

Amy BeberVanzo / Alex Kihurani would not finish the first day.

in the morning and early afternoon of Friday. After a heavy shower at lunchtime, the weather cleared and stayed good for the rest of the event.

The first stage was a short blast around the Yavapai County Fairgrounds and was taken by Hoeck two seconds ahead of Burke and Whitman.

The teams went out to tackle First View North followed by Witty Tom North then reverse direction back to the fairgrounds. Hoeck won First View, adding another three seconds to his lead, though Brian Street / Rob Amato got past Burke into second place. Whitman lost close to five minutes on the stage putting him out of contention.

Burke won Witty Tom North from Whitman and Hoeck; his turn of speed would propel him past Hoeck into first place. The stage would also see the first retirement as Amy BerberVanzo / Alex Kihurani had mechanical problems.

When the teams turned around and repeated the stages back to the fairgrounds it was Burke who established a clear dominance and took all the desert stages. On Witty Tom South he took nine seconds from Hoeck followed by Scott. On First View he took a further nine seconds, this time from George Plsek / Jeff Burmeister. Georgakopoulos would retire when he went off the road on Witty Tom South.

In the Fairgrounds Hoeck was fastest again but as the teams drove back to their hotels around Prescott it was Burke leading the field from Plsek by thirty-four seconds with Scott and Hoeck close by. Leading the two-wheel drive classes were Kristopher Marciniak / Christine Wittish in their Dodge Neon.

Day two continued the fight between the four leaders. The day would start in the fairgrounds then

Jennifer Imai / Sameer Parekh check into a control.

*Right: Doug Chernis /
Craig Macnair at dusk.*

Below: Brad Morris / Pete Morris on the last stage of the event.

Wolfgang Hoeck.

Roger Hull / Sean Gallagher in the fairgrounds

Mustafa Samli / Mike McKittrick in their Mitsubishi Galant.

go out to Perkinsville for seven stages through the day, finishing with a final visit to the fairgrounds.

Whitman would not start the day—retiring due to ongoing electrical problems. Scott took the first stage from Hoeck and Plsek. Then in a repeat of Friday, Burke took the first two desert stages—First View North and Perkinsville West—from Scott and Hoeck, then Hoeck and Scott.

After a service break, the teams went up and down the Limestone Canyon road with Plsek winning both directions from Burke and Scott. Then it was back to Perkinsville where Burke scored another two wins. On this running of Witty Tom South, Lisa Klassen / Alan Perry suffered a major roll. Though both driver and co-driver were unhurt the car was definitely retired.

The sting in the tail of the event was a single stage of over twenty miles that had been created by joining the Perkinsville and First View stages. By this time, Burke had built a lead of more than one minute so he did not need to win the stage just get a good time. He did this coming in six seconds behind stage-winner Scott.

The final run of the Fairgrounds Special stage was taken by Hoeck from Scott and Burke but the stage times would not affect the overall results.

When the event results were posted, Marciniak / Wittish had won the Stock class and were the first two-wheel drive team home; Street / Amato won the Group N class.

Overall, Burke / Beavis won the event two minutes ahead of second-placed Scott / Dillon. Hoeck / O'Hanlon came third—thus Hoeck surrendered his lead in the championship to Burke.

Mike Whitman / Bill Westrick enter their Ford Escort Cosworth.

But with a mere five points separating the two drivers, the championship was still entirely open to the last event.

Above: Lisa Klassen / Alan Perry were making good time . . .

Prescott Rally - Schedule

Stage #	First Car	Stage Name	Miles
Friday - October 6			
		Rally Start	
1	15:39	Fairgrounds Sprint 1	0.6
2	17:03	First View North 1	11.3
3	17:25	Witty Tom North	7.7
		Service	
4	19:32	Witty Tom South 1	7.7
5	19:50	First View South	11.2
6	20:53	Fairgrounds Sprint 2	0.6
Saturday - October 7			
7	8:59	Fairgrounds Sprint 3	0.6
8	10:03	First View North 2	11.9
9	10:23	Perkinsville West 1	11.4
		Service	
10	12:05	Limestone Canyon North	3.9
11	13:30	Limestone Canyon South	3.8
12	14:02	Witty Tom South 2	7.8
13	14:19	Perkinsville West 2	11.4
		Service	
14	16:41	Perkins View	21.3
15	18:03	Fairgrounds Sprint 4	0.6
		Rally Finish	

. . . until they rolled on Witty Tom South.

Leon Styles / Tracy Manspeaker slide through the cut.

Prescott Rally - Results

POSITION							
O'all	Class	Class	Car #	Driver	Co-Driver	Car	TOTAL
1	1	O4	25	Seamus Burke	Chrissie Beavis	Mitsubishi Evo 8	96:31
2	2	O4	96	Brian Scott	John Dillon	Subaru WRX	98:38
3	3	O4	89	Wolfgang Hoeck	Piers O'Hanlon	Mitsubishi Evo VII	98:42
4	1	S	761	Kristopher Marciniak	Christine Wittish	Dodge Neon	127:34
5	1	GN	13	Brian Street	Rob Amato	Mitsubishi Evo 6	135:12
		O4	30	George Plsek	Jeff Burmeister	Mitsubishi Evo	DNF
		O4	73	Mike Whitman	Bill Westrick	Ford Escort RS Cosworth	DNF
		O4	88	George Georgakopoulos	Faruq Mays	Subaru Impreza	DNF
		O4	14	Amy BeberVanzo	Alex Kihurani	Mitsubishi Evo 8	DNF

Regional Event Entrants

O4	356	Doug Chernis	Craig Macnair	Subaru WRX STI
PS	343	Tim Moser	Dick Moser	VW Golf GTI
O4	776	Lisa Klassen	Alan Perry	Mitsubishi Evo
G2	374	Leon Styles	Tracy Manspeaker	Ford Escort
O4	37	Jeff Register	Duncan Smith	Subaru Impreza
PS	792	George Doganis	Tom Smith	Nissan Sentra SE-R
G5	303	Roger Hull	Sean Gallagher	Plymouth Laser RS
G2	43	Brad Morris	Pete Morris	Mitsubishi Lancer
GT	320	Zach Heidepriem	Shea Burns	Subaru Legacy
G2	695	Larry Gross	Doug Young	Toyota Corolla
PS	315	Paula Gibeault	Terry Stonecipher	VW Jetta
O4	310	Mustafa Samli	Mike McKittrick	Mitsubishi Galant
G2	709	Chuck Wilson	John Black	Nissan Pickup
G2	446	Jennifer Imai	Sameer Parekh	Suzuki Swift GT
GT	39	Scott Clark	Marie Boyd	Subaru
G2	845	John Sundelin	Ken Cassidy	Ford Focus
PS	301	Tony Chavez	Steven Taylor	VW Golf GTI

Brian Street / Rob Amato would take first in Group N.

Right, above: Wolfgang Hoeck / Piers O'Hanlon on their way to third overall.

Right, below: Tim Moser / Dick Moser enter the regional event.

Below: Brad Morris / Pete Morris.

Lake Superior Performance Rally (LSPR)
Houghton, Michigan
October 20–21, 2006

As the teams headed to the Upper Peninsula of Michigan for the penultimate round of the Rally America Championship, Travis Pastrana held a commanding lead in the overall standings and just needed a sixth-place finish to take the championship. Only Matt Iorio was still in contention, but some way behind and would have to win this event to keep his hopes alive.

The Subaru team had entered Travis Pastrana / Christian Edstrom and Ken Block / Alex Gelsomino. Both drivers have been trained by Tim O'Neil who was entered in his first event for two years with co-driver Martin Headland. Iorio was to be co-driven by regular Ole Holter. He had loaned his second car to Dave Anton / Robbie Durant to try their hands at an Open Class car— Anton having already sewn up the Group N championship for the year.

Mitsubishi entries were headed by Andrew Comrie-Picard (ACP) / Marc Goldfarb and Chris Gilligan / Joe Peterson.

Left: Matthew Johnson / Kim DeMotte on their way to the PGT championship.

Above: Ken Block / Alex Gelsomino win LSPR.

Above: Mark Utecht at Parc Exposé

PGT regulars Tanner Foust / Scott Crouch had not got their Subaru back on the road after their crash in Colorado and were not in attendance. This allowed Matthew Johnson to seal the class championship just by starting the event with his co-driver Kim DeMotte. Kenny Bartram, with co-driver Dennis Hotson, had a similar situation—taking the Production championship just by starting the event.

The event was run over two days but the stages would be compressed into a challenging twenty-five hours of competition. On the Friday evening and night, the teams would compete in the southerly stages of the Ottawa National Forest around L'Anse and Kenton. Saturday stages were to the north—on the Keweenaw.

Snow left behind from a storm in the previous week lined the roads and, although it did not stick, the Friday night gave the drivers some falling snow to challenge the visibility. On Saturday it remained cold, not getting out of the low forties throughout, but stayed dry for the event.

The first stage—Herman—was taken by Block from Iorio and Pastrana. Already the event had lost one of the front runners when ACP hit a rock and had to retire. Then, on stage 2, the championship was decided when Iorio slid off the road and rolled. His car was damaged too much to be able to continue and he retired, thus putting Pastrana in an unassailable position for the championship. The stage was taken by O'Neil showing his students the way by beating Block by a full twenty seconds.

The night would consist of a further five stages and O'Neil and Pastrana would swap fastest times with Block always in contention. By the end of the

Below: Tim O'Neil / Martin Headland took second overall.

Not many stages cross live railway tracks (Bruce Davis / Jimmy Brandt).

Matt Huuki / Josh VanDenHeuvel compete in the regional event.

Below: Andrew Comrie-Picard.

Below: Ken Block / Alex Gelsomino.

night Pastrana was leading Block by nineteen seconds with O'Neil another fourteen behind.

The second day continued the fight among Block, Pastrana and O'Neil. Block came out hard taking stage 8 (Gratiot Lake) from Pastrana and Anton. Then on the next stage, Anton had to retire when he headed for the scenery and ended with all four wheels off the road. The stage was won by Block—this time from O'Neil and Pastrana. Stage

Kenny Bartram / Dennis Hotson win Production class.

Martin Headland (L) and Tim O'Neil.

LSPR - Schedule

Stage #	First Car	Stage Name	Miles
Friday - October 20			
	15:15	Rally Start	
1	16:28	Herman	7.21
2	18:00	Bob Lake 1	6.70
3	18:39	Echo Lake 1	4.79
		Service - Kenton	
4	20:22	Passmore 1	17.06
5	21:31	Bob Lake 2	6.70
6	22:10	Echo Lake 2	4.79
		Service - Kenton	
7	23:23	Passmore 2	17.06
Saturday - October 21			
8	11:24	Gratiot Lake 1	8.20
9	12:02	Delaware 1	4.28
10	12:35	Burma 1	4.55
		Service - Copper Harbor	
11	13:42	Brockway Mountain 1	3.16
		Service - Copper Harbor	
12	15:33	Brockway Mountain 2	3.16
		Service - Copper Harbor	
13	16:45	Burma 2	4.60
14	17:19	Delaware 2	4.27
15	17:52	Gratiot Lake 2	8.13
	19:16	Rally Finish	

10, the last before lunch, went to Pastrana from Block.

After lunch, the teams took two runs at the notorious jumps of Brockway Mountain. Block took both runs with Pastrana and O'Neil behind him.

Despite Block's fast times, Pastrana pulled into the final service of the event with a seventeen-second advantage over him. Pastrana's championship was secure but, for a Subaru team one-two, Block needed a good result from this event and from the season closer in December. In the final three stages, Block / Gelsomino found the speed required to take the stage wins and get first overall. O'Neil / Headland also slipped past Pastrana into second place for the event. Pastrana / Edstrom finished third.

Class wins went to Johnson / DeMotte (PGT), Jonathan Bottoms / Carolyn Bosley (Group N), Cary Kendall / Scott Friberg (Group 5), Kenny Bartram / Dennis Hotson (Production) and James Robinson / Andrew Jessup (Group 2).

Miles Bothee / Benjamin Slocum enter their Jetta in Group 2.

Craig Walli / Jonah Liubakka miss the Mine Tour.

Above: Doug Shepherd / Pete Gladysz muddy the great paintwork.

Below: Michael Gagnon / Robert Martin win Production class on day one.

Lake Superior Performance Rally - Results

POSITION O'all	POSITION Class	Class	Car #	Driver	Co-Driver	Car	TOTAL
1	1	O	43	Ken Block	Alessandro Gelsomino	Subaru Impreza WRX STI	1:32:37.0
2	2	O	29	Tim O'Neil	Martin Headland	Subaru STI	1:33:01.7
3	3	O	199	Travis Pastrana	Christian Edstrom	Subaru Impreza WRX STI	1:33:07.7
4	4	O	27	Chris Gilligan	Joe Peterson	Mitsubishi Evo IV	1:36:47.0
5	1	PGT	46	Matthew Johnson	Kim DeMotte	Subaru WRX	1:36:51.4
6	1	GN	91	Jonathan Bottoms	Carolyn Bosley	Subaru WRX STI	1:39:48.4
7	5	O	122	Dennis Martin	Alexander Kihurani	Mitsubishi Lancer Evo IV	1:40:23.4
8	6	O	52	Doug Shepherd	Pete Gladysz	Mitsubishi Eclipse	1:41:22.3
9	7	O	44	Henry Krolikowski	Cynthia Krolikowski	Subaru Impreza	1:41:56.9
10	2	PGT	67	Bryan Pepp	Jerry Stang	Subaru WRX	1:44:05.3
11	1	G5	26	Cary Kendall	Scott Friberg	Dodge SRT-4	1:44:19.3
12	3	PGT	59	Patrick Moro	Mike Rossey	Subaru WRX	1:46:33.0
13	1	P	690	Kenny Bartram	Dennis Hotson	Volkswagen Beetle	1:54:23.5
14	8	O	521	Chris Czyzio	Jeff Secor	Mitsubishi GSX	1:56:09.3
15	1	G2	572	James Robinson	Andrew Jessup	Honda Civic Si	1:56:21.7
16	2	GN	151	Josh Chang	Jeff Cruzan	Subaru WRX	1:57:42.8
17	2	G5	92	Paul Dunn	Bill Westrick	Dodge SRT-4	1:59:26.4
18	2	P	534	Eric Heitkamp	Nick Lehner	Acura RSX	2:00:20.1
		O	100	David Anton	Robbie Durant	Subaru Impreza	DNF
		G5	60	Bruce Davis	Jimmy Brandt	Dodge Neon SRT-4	DNF
		P	98	Mike Merbach	Jeff Feldt	Volkswagon Jetta	DNF
		O	18	Matthew Iorio	Ole Holter	Subaru Impreza	DNF
		O	20	Andrew Comrie-Picard	Marc Goldfarb	Mitsubishi Lancer EVO IV	DNF
		O	507	Micah Wiitala	Jason Takkunen	Subaru Impreza	DNF
		G2	93	Robert Olson	Ryan Johnson	Mazda RX-8	DNF

Regional Event Entrants

Class	Car #	Driver	Co-Driver	Car
O	64	Robert Borowicz	Mariusz Borowicz	Subaru Impreza WRX STI
O	550	Kyle Sarasin	Stuart Sarasin	Subaru Impreza
PGT	523	Travis Hanson	Terry Hanson	2002 Subaru WRX
O	614	Piotr Wiktokczyk	John Nordlie	Subaru Impreza
G5	83	Mark Utecht	Rob Bohn	Ford Mustang
O	570	Erik Payeur	Adam Payeur	Mitsubishi Galant
G2	744	Paul Koll	Matthew Wappler	Volkswagen Golf GTI
O	566	Matt Huuki	Josh VanDenHeuvel	Eagle Talon
O	810	Erick Murray	Nicole Nelson	Subaru Legacy Sport
G2	572	James Robinson	Andrew Jessup	Honda Civic Si
O	622	Larry Parker	Mandi Gentry	Mitsubishi VR4
G2	562	Brian Dondlinger	Dave Parps	Nissan Sentra SE-r
P	480	Michael Gagnon	Robert Martin	Ford Focus ZX3
O	558	James Cox	Scott Parrott	Cherolet S10
P	534	Eric Heitkamp	Nick Lehner	Acura RSX
O	533	Paul Ritchie	Drew Ritchie	Mitsubishi Eclipse GSX
G2	687	Chad Eixenberger	Jay Luikart	Volkswagen GTI
G2	527	Craig Walli	Jonah Liubakka	Saturn SL-2
G2	319	Chris Greenhouse	Matt	Plymouth Neon
G2	478	Evan Moen	Daniel Victor	Acura Integra Type R
G5	555	Colin McCleery	Nancy McCleery	Ford Sierra
P	811	Jaroslaw Sozanski	Kazimierz Pudelek	Subaru Impreza
G2	770	Miles Bothee	Benjamin Slocum	Volkswagen Jetta
G2	548	Matt Bushore	Andrew Bushore	Volkswagen Jetta
G2	734	Thomas Diehl	Mike Rodriquez	Ford Probe GT
G2	569	John Hruska	Carl Seidel	Volkswagen Golf GTI
G2	654	David Grenwis	Corey Voight	Volkswagen GTI
G2	637	Christopher Gordon	Matt Pekuri	Honda CRX
PGT	686	Heath Nunnemacher	Chris Coughlin	Subaru WRX
O	78	Marek Podoluch	Mariusz Malik	Subaru Impreza
G5	591	David Cizmas	Matt Himes	Mazda RX-7
G2	722	Robert Stroik	Ross Wegge	Nissan Sentra
O	774	Otis Dimiters	Alan Ockwell	Subaru Impreza

Above: Colin McCleery / Nancy McCleery lock up on landing.

*Left: Bryan Pepp / Jerry
Stang overshoot on Gratiot
Lake.*

Below: Travis Pastrana / Christian Edstrom take third place.

Laughlin International Rally

Laughlin, Nevada

November 10–12, 2006

Todd Moberly / Ray Moberly win their first national championship event.

Left: Wolfgang Hoeck / Piers O'Hanlon lock their championship second place.

After eight years of support from the Ramada Express Hotel and Casino, the rally, based in Laughlin, Nevada, grew up and expanded this year. First, the whole City of Laughlin took over as event sponsor, then the organizers created a "Motorsports Festival" by adding Drifting and Autocross to the established mix of Performance Rally, GPS Adventure and car shows.

As the action was still scheduled to fit into three days it would make a busy weekend for competitors and organizers alike. The event had also been brought forward in the calendar by three weeks so the risk of bad weather was reduced and indeed temperatures were always comfortable with clear blue skies on all days.

The performance rally competition was spread over three days. Day one would take the teams south to Wikieup, Arizona, for fifty miles of stages. Day two was centered on the Grand Canyon roads around Peach Springs, Arizona. The final day would offer three runs at the Super Stage located behind the main casino drag of Laughlin.

Seamus Burke / Chrissie Beavis were leading until their engine started to give problems.

Jeff Register / Duncan Smith cut the desert on the Super Stage.

Seamus Burke, co-driven by Chrissie Beavis, started with a five-point lead in the championship over Wolfgang Hoeck / Piers O'Hanlon, both teams driving Mitsubishis.

Brian Scott still had an outside chance to win the championship but had not entered the event so would have to settle for no better than third.

Other entries included George Plsek / Jeff Burmeister (Mitsubishi Evo), Mike Whitman / Bill Westrick (Ford Escort Cosworth) and Lauchlin O'Sullivan / John Dillon, who had brought their Mitsubishi Eclipse back from retirement. Subaru entries were led by Todd Moberly / Raymond Moberly, Wyeth Gubelmann / Cindy Krolikowski and George Georgakopoulos / Faruq Mays. After her major roll at Prescott, Lisa Klassen and her team had worked long hours to rebuild the car and get it on the road again in time for Laughlin. At this event she would be co-driven by Mike Jones.

The first day started with a run on the Super Stage, which was won by Burke. Then the teams moved to the Yellow Pine Ranch, which hosted a spectator area. On the stages, Burke would demonstrate his intentions by winning the fourteen-mile stage by forty seconds over Moberly and Gubelmann. The next stage, 17 Mile Road, was also taken by Burke; this time from Plsek and Randy Dowell / Jonathan Schiller. Kevin Welker / Drew Brashler rolled their Subaru on the stage and Brashler was taken to the local hospital for precautionary checks.

On their way back to Laughlin, the teams would tackle the two desert stages in reverse. Whitman won 17 Mile Road and Burke took Cane Springs despite reporting fuel pressure problems. As they completed the long drive back from

Dust would hang in the air for five minutes making driving conditions difficult.

Mike Whitman / Bill Westrick would retire with a blown turbo.

Left: Jeff Rados / Guido Hamacher loses time on stage 7.

Right: Jeff Burmeister prepares himself for the next stage.

Kingman, Burke was leading Gubelmann by more than thirty seconds with Moberly and Plsek behind.

Day two would use two Grand Canyon roads to create the Black Canyon and Diamond Creek stages. Each stage would be driven in then all teams would turn around and drive out. This arrangement had been used in the past but on this occasion it caused some delays when the sweep teams had to deal with accidents.

Burke took the first stage from Plsek and Moberly. Whitman had had turbo problems at the end of the previous night's stages and he was forced to retire when the replacement unit expired. On the way out of Black Canyon it was Plsek who won from Hoeck and Gubelmann. Burke's fuel pressure problem continued from the previous day and would put him out of contention for the win. His goal became an effort to keep going and secure the championship. When the teams got to Diamond Creek, the air was so still that dust could

Jeff Register and Duncan Smith.

Jimmy Keeney / Melissa Salas were the first two-wheel-drive car home.

Street / Amato battle with Georgakopoulos / Mays on the Super Stage.

hang for over five minutes. It gave Burke, running first on the road a distinct advantage on which he capitalized by coming first on the way in—just a few seconds ahead of Plsek and Gubelmann. On the way out, the organizers allowed two-minute intervals. But the uphill road was too much for Burke's ailing car. He was four minutes behind the fastest times for the stage. It was Moberly, who had been lying in fourth overall, who put everything into the stage and came out of the canyon lying first overall

Michael Taylor / Steven Taylor won the Stock class.

Laughlin International Rally - Schedule

Stage #	First Car	Stage Name	Miles
Friday - November 10			
	9:01	Rally Start	
1	9:01	Super Stage	2.0
2	10:46	Yellow Pine Ranch	14.5
		Service - Wikieup	
3	12:39	17 Mile Road West	10.4
4	13:58	17 Mile Road East	10.4
		Service - Wikieup	
5	16:01	Cane Springs	14.5
Saturday - November 11			
6	9:33	Black Canyon North	16.0
7	11:00	Black Canyon South	16.0
		Service - Peach Springs	
8	13:32	Diamond Creek Down	16.8
9	15:05	Diamond Creek Up	16.8
Sunday - November 12			
10	10:00	Super Stage 2	2.0
11	12:00	Super Stage 3	2.0
12	14:00	Super Stage 4	2.0
	14:04	Rally Finish	

Lauchlin O'Sullivan / John Dillon run through the Yellow Pine Ranch.

Even drifters can get air.

Wyeth Gubelmann / Cindy Krolikowski work their way toward the Grand Canyon.

ahead of Gubelmann, Plsek and Hoeck. Burke dropped to fifth overall.

The Sunday stages, with just six miles of competition, could still affect the overall results—and have done so in past years. Burke's car was back on song and he took joint first with Plsek on two of the stages—the first one being won by Plsek from Hoeck. But Moberly drove with enough speed and control to maintain his first position and win the event. In fact none of the top five positions changed on the Sunday.

Laughlin International Rally - Results

National O'all	Class	Class	Car #	Driver	Co-Driver	Car	Total H:M:S
1	1	04	6	Todd Moberly	Raymond Moberly	Subaru WRX STi	1:52:16
2	1	GN	8	Wyeth Gubelmann	Cindy Krolikowski	Subaru WRX STi	1:52:45
3	2	04	3	George Plsek	Jeff Burmeister	Mitsubishi Evo	1:52:48
4	3	04	2	Wolfgang Hoeck	Piers O'Hanlon	Mitsubishi Evo VII	1:53:51
5	4	04	1	Seamus Burke	Chrissie Beavis	Mitsubishi Evo 8	1:54:26
6	1	SS	24	Nathan Conley	Brandye Monks	Subaru WRX Wagon	2:04:08
7	1	02	19	Jimmy Keeney	Melissa Salas	Honda Civic	2:06:40
8	2	02	16	Larry Gross	Doug Young	Toyota Corolla	2:16:16
9	2	GN	31	Craig Studnicky	Jeff Hagan	Mitsubishi Evo 6	2:17:24
10	3	02	12	Bruce Davis	Jimmy Brandt	Dodge Neon SRT-4	2:20:05
11	5	04	18	George Georgakopoulos	Faruq Mays	Subaru Impreza	2:21:39
12	1	S	23	Michael Taylor	Steven Taylor	Ford Ranger	2:28:25
13	4	02	26	Lars Wolfe	Scot Langford	VW Jetta	2:29:59
14	6	04	7	Randy Dowell	Jonathan Schiller	Mitsubishi Mirage	2:34:29
15	3	GN	27	Brian Street	Rob Amato	Mitsubishi Evo 6	2:41:46
16	2	S	22	Kristopher Marciniak	Christine Wittish	Dodge Neon	2:50:49
17	5	02	13	Jeff Rados	Guido Hamacher	Ford Ranger	3:19:29
		02	28	Andrew Lockhart	Robin Lockhart	Honda	DNF
		SS	5	Lauchlin O'Sullivan	John Dillon	Mitsubishi Eclipse	DNF
		04	4	Mike Whitman	Bill Westrick	Ford Escort RS	DNF
		02	29	Brad Morris	Ryan Gutile	Mitsubishi Lancer	DNF

Regional Rally Entrants

9	Jeff Register	Duncan Smith	Subaru Impreza STi
14	Marvin Ronquillo	John Burke	Subaru WRX
15	George Doganis	Tom Smith	Nissan Sentra SE-R
10	Lisa Klassen	Mike Jones	Mitsubishi Evo 6
21	Sarkis Mazmanian	Michael Mazmanian	Acura Integra
36	Brian Hamblin	Mike Hamblin	Volvo 240
33	Joshua Milos	Michael Milos	GMC Sonoma
35	Chuck Wilson	John Black	Nissan Pickup
37	Jennifer Imai	Jeff Dubrule	Suzuki Swift GT
34	Scott Clark	Marie Boyd	Subaru
30	John Crowningshield	Rosie Ramirez	VW Golf GTi
11	Tim Moser	Dick Moser	VW Golf GTi
38	Kevin Welker	Drew Brashler	Subaru Impreza
20	Ken Gushi	Tsukasa Gushi	Subaru Impreza

The overall win went to Moberly / Moberly from Gubelmann / Krolikowski, who also took the Group N class, and Plsek / Burmeister. Class wins went to Nathan Conley / Brandye Monks in Super Stock, Jimmy Keeney / Melissa Salas in Open 2wd and Michael Taylor / Steven Taylor in Stock.

The championship had been wrapped up with Seamus Burke winning the driver's championship from Wolfgang Hoeck and Chrissie Beavis winning the co-driver's championship from Piers O'Hanlon.

Class wins for driver and co-driver went to Bruce Davis and Jimmy Brandt in two-wheel drive, Brian Street and Rob Amato Group N, Kristopher Marciniak and Christine Wittish in Stock. In Super Stock there was a three-way tie shared by drivers Brian Street, Dennis Chizma and Nathan Conley; and co-drivers Andrew Cushman, Brandye Monks and David Weiman.

Todd Moberly (R) / Raymond Moberly celebrate their win.

Below: George Plsek / Jeff Burmeister are third overall.

Wild West Rally
Olympia, Washington
December 2–3, 2006

The Wild West Rally proved to have been named accurately when it was held in the week following the wettest month on record. To add insult to injury, the Monday before the event, the region was hit by a blizzard that brought the area to a standstill. Some local commuters took six hours to get home in the snow and at 3:00 A.M. there were still leftover traffic jams from the rush hour.

For the organizers, months of detailed planning were washed away when the owners of the forest withdrew their permission to use the roads. Their reason was concern over the underlying condition of the sodden tracks and the effect that the high-speed competition would have on them. With just three days to go to the event, and many competitors already traveling, John Forespring and his team had to face a major challenge.

Fortunately, Grays Harbor County and Pacific Raceways came to the rescue and an event was organized consisting of a day of competition at the Straddleline ORV Park followed by a day of competition at the raceway.

Even with this generous last-minute help there

Left: Travis Pastrana / Christian Edstrom complete their season with a win at Wild West.

Above: Pat Richard (co-driven by Mark Williams) takes second place on his only outing of the season.

Victor Bartosek / Don Flagg clip a cone on their first run round Pacific Raceways.

were still problems. The ORV Park, held on Saturday, was a mud bath over a foot deep in places. At the outset, even the organizers were having difficulty getting round the course though it did dry out as the day went on and the teams completed five stages of one lap each.

At the raceway, there would be three stages of three laps each. Four cars were put on the track at a time with a fifteen-second gap between each car. The teams would have to run the asphalt using gravel tires.

With many of the championship positions already decided, the overall entry was down with many teams staying at home to start preparation for the next year—the most significant example being Matt Iorio. Lying second in the championship and leading Ken Block by one point, his absence meant that Block only had to start to take second place in the championship.

Open four-wheel drive entries came from the Subaru Rally USA team of Travis Pastrana / Christian Edstrom and Ken Block / Alex Gelsomino. Reigning champion, Pat Richard had come down from his hometown of Squamish to compete for the first time this year. His co-driver would be Mark Williams. Local sibling team of Dave Hintz / Rick Hintz would round out the open class entrants. At the last minute, Jamie Thomas upgraded from a regional entry to national and would be co-driven by Kim DeMotte. In two-wheel drive, Bruce Davis / Jimmy Brandt and Sans Thompson / David Stone had entered Dodge Neons. Matt

Peter Barnes / Ronald Crawford enter their Nissan Sentra.

Jamie Thomas / Kim DeMotte
get their time on stage 4.

Paul Eklund / Jeff Price win
the first regional event.

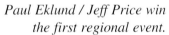

Below: Kris Dahl / Edward Dahl on the track.

Conditions are so tough even the Zero car requires assistance.

Ken Block / Alex Gelsomino entertain the crowd at ORV.

Christensen / Eric Christensen had entered an Acura RSX and Kenny Bartram / Dennis Hotson were out in their VW Beetle.

Pastrana demonstrated how his driving had matured over the season by taking the first three stages despite the terrible conditions. Close behind were Richard then Block and Hintz. The top four benefited from their four-wheel drive and were a clear ten seconds faster than the two-wheel drive teams.

On stage 4, the top three times were swapped with Block coming first followed by Richard and Pastrana. By the time the teams went out for the final run of the day, the mud had dried out somewhat and the cars were able to make some headway. Richard took the stage by a tenth of a second from Pastrana and Block.

At the end of day one, Pastrana was leading from Richard by three seconds. Block was a further seven behind, then Hintz. Davis was leading the two-wheel drive contenders.

When the teams moved to the raceway for the second day of competition, Richard would have a challenge to compete with the works teams in his older and less powerful Impreza. On the first stage of the day, Pastrana won by six seconds from Block then Richard. The second time around it was Block just half a second ahead of Pastrana and almost three seconds ahead of Richard.

With one more stage at the raceway, Pastrana / Edstrom had a clear lead of fifteen seconds that they extended in the final stage. Block / Gelsomino had caught up to be just half a second behind Ri-

Sheldon hosts the teams for Parc Exposé.

Wild West Rally - Schedule

Stage #	First Car	Stage Name	Miles
Saturday - December 2			
	10:00	Rally Start	
1	10:10	ORV Park 1	0.70
2	11:32	ORV Park 2	0.70
3	13:05	ORV Park 3	0.70
4	13:43	ORV Park 4	0.70
5	14:45	ORV Park 5	0.70
Sunday - December 3			
6	12:10	Pacific Raceways 1	6.75
7	13:18	Pacific Raceways 2	6.75
8	14:43	Pacific Raceways 3	6.75
	14:50	Rally Finish	

Sans Thompson / David Stone win Group 2.

chard / Williams, but Richard did enough to keep his second place.

Davis / Brandt were the first two-wheel drive home, taking the Group 5 class as well. Thomas / DeMotte came first in the Production GT class and Thompson / Stone won the Group 2.

In the championship race, Pastrana had already clinched the overall and open class wins. His third place at Wild West secured Block the runner-up championship—thus giving the Subaru Rally Team a one-two result from their first season back in American rallying. Iorio would have to settle for third.

The Group N and Production GT championships had been resolved at LSPR. Group N was taken by David Anton from Jonathan Bottoms and Production GT by Matthew Johnson from Tanner Foust.

Cars line up at the ORV Park.

*Pat Richard / Mark Williams
in the ORV Park.*

In two-wheel drive, the Woodner cup was won by Kenny Bartram, one point ahead of Bruce Davis. Bartram won the Production Class championship from Kathy Jarvis, Davis won Group 5 from Cary Kendall and Eric Duncan held Group 2 from Sans Thompson.

Wild West Rally - Results

POSITION O/A	Class	Class	Car #	Driver	Co-Driver	Car	Total
1	1	O	199	Travis Pastrana	Christian Edstrom	Subaru Impreza	24:59.3
2	2	O	1	Patrick Richard	Mark Williams	Subaru Impreza	25:16.9
3	3	O	43	Ken Block	Alessandro Gelsomino	Subaru Impreza WRX STi	25:17.9
4	4	O	207	Dave Hintz	Rick Hintz	Subaru WRX	26:23.6
5	1	G5	60	Bruce Davis	Jimmy Brandt	Dodge Neon SRT-4	27:34.7
6	1	PGT	215	Jamie Thomas	Kim DeMotte	Subaru WRX Wagon	27:53.8
7	1	G2	49	Sans Thompson	David Stone	Dodge Neon	29:04.9
8	2	G2	144	Matt Chrstensen	Eric Christensen	Acura RSX	30:02.1
9	3	G2	690	Kenny Bartram	Dennis Hotson	VW Beetle	53:21.0

Regional Event Entrants

O	233	Paul Eklund	Jeff Price	Subaru WRX STi
O	207	Dave Hintz	Rick Hintz	Subaru WRX
O	294	Barrett Dash	Tracy Manspeaker	Subaru 22 Brighton
O	260	Terry Christensen	Benjamin Bradley	Subaru Impreza 2.5RS
O	438	Victor Bartosek	Don Flagg	Audi Quattro
PGT	271	Matthew Tabor	Jeffrey Zurschmeide	Subaru Impreza 2.5RS
O	424	Mark Mager	Miller Dumaoal	Subaru Legacy Sport
PGT	502	Matthew Milner	John Taylor	Subaru Legacy
P	258	Kris Dahl	K Edward Dahl	Acura Integra
G2	439	Garth Ankeny	Russ Kraushaar	Saab 96
O	433	Mitchell Williams	Alix Hakala	Subaru Impreza
G2	692	Peter Barnes	Ronald Crawford	Nissan Sentra
G2	251	Lou Beck	Randee Hahn	Ford Focus
O	447	Christopher Baldini	Kailee Wheeler	Mazda 323 GTX
G2	240	Chris Blakely	Ian Pinter	VW GTi
P	474	Marcus Song	Brandon Harer	Chevy Turbo Sprint
P	231	Kristen Tabor	Janice Tabor	Nissan Sentra SE-R
O	459	Pat Harris	Tim Maple	Mazda GTX
P	232	Mark Tabor	Doug Heredos	Acura RSX Type S
G2	132	April Smith	Johdi Mastermon	VW Golf

*Anyone want a mud bath?
(Marcus Song / Brandon Harer).*

Dave Hintz / Rick Hintz win the second regional event.

Kenny Bartram wins a bet by sporting a half mustache.

Mark Mager / Miller Dumaoal in their Subaru Legacy

Travis Pastrana and Christian Edstrom (shown at LSPR) win the Rally America driver's and co-driver's championships.

Rally America Championship

Final Standings

Overall Position

	Driver					Co-driver		
Position	**Name**	**From**	**Total Points**		**Position**	**Name**	**From**	**Total Points**
1	Travis Pastrana	Davidsonville, Md.	137		1	Christian Edstrom	New York, N.Y.	137
2	Ken Block	Rancho Santa Fe, Calif.	90		2	Alessandro Gelsomino	Santa Clarita, Calif.	90
3	Matthew Iorio	Westmoreland, N.H.	77		3	Ole Holter	Long Beach, Calif.	77
4	Matthew Johnson	Apex, N.C.	57		4	Kim DeMotte	St Louis, Mo.	60
5	Andrew Pinker	Perth, Aus.	52		5	Robbie Durant	Oxfordshire, England	53
6	Andrew Comrie-Picard	Edmonton, Alb. Can.	50		6	Massimo Daddoveri	Lucca	41
7	Alfredo DeDominicis	Teramo	42		6	Joe Petersen	Mayville, Wis.	41
8	Chris Gilligan	Cornelius, N.C.	41		8	Cynthia Krolikowski	Wyandotte, Mich.	37
9	Tanner Foust	Steamboat Springs, Colo.	37		9	Scott Crouch	Boulder, Colo.	34
10	David Anton	Mount Laurel, N.J.	28		10	Rod Hendricksen	Clinton, N.J.	30
11	Robert Olson	Eden Prairie, Minn.	25		11	Marc Goldfarb	Atkinson, N.H.	29
12	Kenny Bartram	Stillwater, Okla.	24		12	Mark Williams	N Potomac, Md.	28
13	Eric Langbein	Annapolis, Md.	23		13	Jimmy Brandt	Lake Odessa, Mich.	26
13	Bruce Davis	Granite Bay, Calif.	23		14	Jeremy Wimpey	Blacksburg, Va.	24
15	Henry Krolikowski	Wyandotte, Mich.	22		14	Dominik Jozwiak	Ridgewood, N.Y.	24
15	Ramana Lagemann	Somerville, Mass.	22		14	Dennis Hotson	Stillwater, Okla.	24
17	Otis Dimiters	Great Neck, N.Y.	19		17	Martin Headland	Caledon, Ont. Can.	23
18	Patrick Moro	Dublin, Ohio	17		18	Ryan Johnson	Winona, Minn.	22
18	Patrick Richard	Squamish, B.C. Can.	17		18	Michael Fennell	Kingston	22
18	Tim O'Neil	Dalton, N.H.	17		20	Alan Ockwell	Stouffville, Ont. Can.	19
21	Dave Hintz	Enumclaw, Wash.	16		21	Alexander Kihurani	Mohnton, Pa.	18
21	Thomas Lawless	Yonkers, N.Y.	16		22	Carolyn Bosley	Hinesburg, Vt.	16
21	Jonathan Bottoms	Buffalo, N.Y.	16		22	Rick Hintz	El Cajon, Calif.	16
24	Wyeth Gubelmann	Placerville, Colo.	15		24	Jeffrey Burmeister	St Louis Park, Minn.	14
25	Lauchlin O'Sullivan	San Francisco, Calif.	14		24	Scott Putnam	Richfield, Minn.	14
26	Eric Duncan	Soda Springs, Idaho	12		26	John Dillon	Thousand Oaks, Calif.	12
26	Amy BeberVanzo	Petaluma, Calif.	12		26	Matt Duncan	Clarkston, Mich.	12
26	Sans Thompson	Grass Valley, Calif.	12		28	Pamela McGarvey	Columbus, Ohio	11
29	Antoine L'Estage	St. Jean, Qc Can.	11		29	Pete Gladysz	Troy, Mich.	10
29	George Plsek Jr	Solana Beach, Calif.	11		29	Scott Friberg	Forest Lake, Minn.	10
31	Doug Shepherd	Plymouth, Mich.	10		31	Jerry Stang	Marquette, Minn.	9
31	Cary Kendall	Forest Lake, Minn.	10		31	Dave Shindle	Falls Church, Va.	9
33	Jon Hamilton	Marysville, Ohio	9		31	Ken Sabo	Marietta, Ga.	9
33	Eric Burmeister	Dearborn Hts, Mich.	9		34	Brian Sharkey	Aaglenhead, Co Louth	8
33	Kathy Jarvis	Park City, Utah	9		34	Alan Perry	Bainbridge Island, Wash.	8
33	Bryan Pepp	Marquette, Mich.	9		36	Keith Morison	Calgary, Alb. Can.	7
37	Jamie Thomas	Kirkland, Wash.	8		36	Mike Rossey	Rochester, Mich.	7

Rally America Championship

Final Standings

<table>
<tr><th colspan="4" style="text-align:center">Driver</th><th colspan="4" style="text-align:center">Co-driver</th></tr>
<tr><th colspan="8" style="text-align:center">Overall Position</th></tr>
<tr><th>Position</th><th>Name</th><th>From</th><th>Total Points</th><th>Position</th><th>Name</th><th>From</th><th>Total Points</th></tr>
<tr><td>38</td><td>Norm LeBlanc</td><td>Pemberton, B.C. Can.</td><td>7</td><td>36</td><td>Jeff Feldt</td><td>Kaukauna, Wis.</td><td>7</td></tr>
<tr><td>38</td><td>Michael Merbach</td><td>Appleton, Wis.</td><td>7</td><td>39</td><td>Christine Beavis</td><td>San Diego, Calif.</td><td>6</td></tr>
<tr><td>40</td><td>Paul Dunn</td><td>Oakley, Ill.</td><td>6</td><td>39</td><td>Bill Westrick</td><td>Royal Oak, Mich.</td><td>6</td></tr>
<tr><td>40</td><td>George Georgakopoulos</td><td>Rockville, Md.</td><td>6</td><td>39</td><td>Marianne Stevens</td><td>Windsor, Ont. Can.</td><td>6</td></tr>
<tr><td>40</td><td>Jim Stevens</td><td>Kingsville, Ont. Can.</td><td>6</td><td>39</td><td>Faruq Mays</td><td>Gaithersburg, Md.</td><td>6</td></tr>
<tr><td>40</td><td>Dennis Martin</td><td>Green Bay, Wis.</td><td>6</td><td>39</td><td>Craig Marr</td><td>Chico, Calif.</td><td>6</td></tr>
<tr><td>40</td><td>Tom Young</td><td>Brighton, Mich.</td><td>6</td><td>39</td><td>Jim LeBeau</td><td>Southfield, Mich.</td><td>6</td></tr>
<tr><td>40</td><td>Brian Scott</td><td>Phoenix, Ariz</td><td>6</td><td>39</td><td>David Stone</td><td>Acme, Mich.</td><td>6</td></tr>
<tr><td>46</td><td>Robin Jones</td><td>Vergennes, Vt.</td><td>5</td><td>46</td><td>William Sekella</td><td>Reading, Pa.</td><td>5</td></tr>
<tr><td>46</td><td>Mark McElduff</td><td>Chicago, Ill.</td><td>5</td><td>46</td><td>Carl Fisher</td><td>Pittsboro, N.C.</td><td>5</td></tr>
<tr><td>46</td><td>Matt Christensen</td><td>Boise, Idaho</td><td>5</td><td>46</td><td>Eric Christensen</td><td>Boise, Idaho</td><td>5</td></tr>
<tr><td>46</td><td>Gary Cavett</td><td>Kirkland, Wash.</td><td>5</td><td>46</td><td>John Nordlie</td><td>Bloomington, Minn.</td><td>5</td></tr>
<tr><td>46</td><td>Greg Drozd</td><td>Lyons, Ill.</td><td>5</td><td>50</td><td>Maciej Sawicki</td><td>Bartlett, Ill.</td><td>4</td></tr>
<tr><td>51</td><td>Wojciech Okula</td><td>Bethel, Ct.</td><td>4</td><td>50</td><td>Lise Mendham</td><td>Lyndeborough, N.H.</td><td>4</td></tr>
<tr><td>51</td><td>Christopher Duplessis</td><td>Mason Twp, Maine</td><td>4</td><td>50</td><td>Edward McNelly</td><td>Oxford, Maine</td><td>4</td></tr>
<tr><td>51</td><td>John Conley</td><td>Monument, Colo.</td><td>4</td><td>50</td><td>Jeff Secor</td><td>Hudsonville, Mich.</td><td>4</td></tr>
<tr><td>51</td><td>Josh Chang</td><td>Allen, Texas</td><td>4</td><td>50</td><td>Jason Takkunen</td><td>Anoka, Minn.</td><td>4</td></tr>
<tr><td>51</td><td>Edward Mendham</td><td>Lyndeborough, N.H.</td><td>4</td><td>50</td><td>Jeff Cruzan</td><td>Allen, Texas</td><td>4</td></tr>
<tr><td>51</td><td>Marcin Kowalski</td><td>Darien, Ill.</td><td>4</td><td>50</td><td>Adam Pelc</td><td>Middle Village, N.Y.</td><td>4</td></tr>
<tr><td>57</td><td>Travis Hanson</td><td>Williamsburg, Mich.</td><td>3</td><td>50</td><td>Rebecca Greek</td><td>Denver, Colo.</td><td>4</td></tr>
<tr><td>57</td><td>James Robinson</td><td>Delaware, Ohio</td><td>3</td><td>50</td><td>Steven Treml</td><td>Colorado Springs, Colo.</td><td>4</td></tr>
<tr><td>57</td><td>Lars Wolfe</td><td>Danville, Calif.</td><td>3</td><td>59</td><td>Keith Boyd</td><td>Enniskillen, Northern Ireland</td><td>3</td></tr>
<tr><td>57</td><td>Jon Nichols</td><td>Pointe-Claire, Q.C. Can.</td><td>3</td><td>59</td><td>Freddy Weil</td><td>Montreal, Q.C. Can.</td><td>3</td></tr>
<tr><td>57</td><td>Chris Rhodes</td><td>Kingwood, Texas</td><td>3</td><td>59</td><td>Russell Norton</td><td>Fairport, N.Y.</td><td>3</td></tr>
<tr><td>57</td><td>Andy Brown</td><td>Phoenix, Ariz.</td><td>3</td><td>59</td><td>William Rhodes</td><td>Haverford, Pa.</td><td>3</td></tr>
<tr><td>57</td><td>Arthur Odero-Jowi</td><td>Arlington, Texas</td><td>3</td><td>59</td><td>Scot Langford</td><td>Springfield, Ore.</td><td>3</td></tr>
<tr><td>57</td><td>Daniel Cook</td><td>Hinesburg, Vt.</td><td>3</td><td>59</td><td>Andrew Jessup</td><td>Raymond, Ohio</td><td>3</td></tr>
<tr><td>57</td><td>Dan Brosnan</td><td>Norwood, Mass.</td><td>3</td><td>59</td><td>Nick Lehner</td><td>Dublin, Ohio</td><td>3</td></tr>
<tr><td>57</td><td>Jean-Louis Weil</td><td>Prevost, Q.C. Can.</td><td>3</td><td>59</td><td>Erik Lee</td><td>Belfast, Maine</td><td>3</td></tr>
<tr><td>57</td><td>Andrew Havas</td><td>Hopewell Junction, N.Y.</td><td>3</td><td>59</td><td>Kathryn Hansen</td><td>Friday Harbor, Wash.</td><td>3</td></tr>
<tr><td>57</td><td>Brendan Kelly</td><td>Jamison, Pa.</td><td>3</td><td>59</td><td>Emily Burton-Weinman</td><td>Minneapolis, Minn.</td><td>3</td></tr>
<tr><td>57</td><td>Ralph Kosmides</td><td>Newport Beach, Calif.</td><td>3</td><td>59</td><td>Duffy Bowers</td><td>Afton, Va.</td><td>3</td></tr>
<tr><td>57</td><td>Eric Heitkamp</td><td>Columbus, Ohio</td><td>3</td><td>59</td><td>Jeffrey Hagan</td><td>Whitby, Ont. Can.</td><td>3</td></tr>
<tr><td>57</td><td>Charles Kothe</td><td>Indianapolis, Ind.</td><td>3</td><td>59</td><td>Terry Hanson</td><td>Williamsburg, Mich.</td><td>3</td></tr>
<tr><td>57</td><td>Michael Hurst</td><td>Pendleton, Ind.</td><td>3</td><td>59</td><td>Carl Schenk</td><td>Ste Anne-de-Bellevue, QC CAN</td><td>3</td></tr>
</table>

Rally America Championship

Final Standings

Overall Position

Position	Driver Name	From	Total Points	Position	Co-driver Name	From	Total Points
57	John Cassidy IV	Bangor, Maine	3	73	Eddie Fries	Yonkers, N.Y.	2
57	Chris Czyzio	Flushing, Mich.	3	73	John Allen	Bainbridge Island, Wash.	2
57	Chip Miller	Snohomish, Wash.	3	75	Chris Stark	Baltimore, Md.	1
76	Timothy Penasack	Nashua, N.H.	2	75	Alexander Korovkine	Framingham, Mass.	1
76	Seamus Burke	Powder Springs, Ga.	2	75	Brandye Monks	Colorado Springs, Colo.	1
76	Peter Reilly	Brampton, Ont. Can.	2	75	David Dooley	Bronx, N.Y.	1
76	Tim Paterson	Issaquah, Wash.	2	75	Noel Gallagher	Yonkers, N.Y.	1
80	Jason Waples	Pueblo, Colo.	1	75	Mariusz Malik	Chicago, Ill.	1
80	Dmitri Kishkarev	Ocean, N.J.	1	75	Nathalie Richard	Halifax, N.S. Can.	1
80	Timothy Stevens	Wells, Maine	1	75	Ray Moberly	Colorado Springs, Colo.	1
80	Kazimierz Pudelek	Chicago, Ill.	1	75	Daniel Sprongl	Mississauga, Can.	1
80	Paul Choiniere II	Shelburne, Vt.	1	75	Jeffrey Becker	New York, N.Y.	1
80	Patrick Lilly	Yonkers, N.Y.	1	75	Ray Felice	Guelph, Ont. Can.	1
80	Daniel O'Brien	Maspeth, N.Y.	1	75	Damien Irwin	Chicago, Ill.	1
80	Joan Hoskinson	Thunder Bay, Ont. Can.	1	75	Phillip Assad	Brampton, Ont. Can.	1
80	Frank Sprongl	Georgetown, Ont. Can.	1	75	Patrick Walsh	Aberystwytli, Corgdigion	1
80	Andrew Sutherland	Studio City, Calif.	1				
80	Eoin McGeough	Memphis, Tenn.	1				
80	Todd Moberly	Pueblo West, Colo.	1				
80	Nathan Conley	Monument, Colo.	1				

2-Wheel Drive (Woodner Cup)

Position	Driver Name	From	Total Points	Position	Co-driver Name	From	Total Points
1	Kenny Bartram	Stillwater, Okla.	84	1	Dennis Hotson	Stillwater, Okla.	84
2	Bruce Davis	Granite Bay, Calif.	83	2	Jimmy Brandt	Lake Odessa, Mich.	83
3	Cary Kendall	Forest Lake, Minn.	57	3	Scott Friberg	Forest Lake, Minn.	57

Rally America Championship

Final Standings

Open Class

Driver					Co-driver		
Position	Name	From	Total Points	Position	Name	From	Total Points
1	Travis Pastrana	Davidsonville, Md.	137	1	Christian Edstrom	New York, N.Y.	137
2	Ken Block	Rancho Santa Fe, Calif.	92	2	Alessandro Gelsomino	Santa Clarita, Calif.	92
3	Matthew Iorio	Westmoreland, N.H.	81	3	Ole Holter	Long Beach, Calif.	81
4	Chris Gilligan	Cornelius, N.C.	53	4	Joe Petersen	Mayville, Wis.	53
5	Andrew Comrie-Picard	Edmonton, Alb. Can.	50	5	Massimo Daddoveri	Lucca	41
6	Alfredo DeDominicis	Teramo	42	6	Cynthia Krolikowski	Wyandotte, Mich.	37
7	Andrew Pinker	Perth, Aus.	34	7	Robbie Durant	Oxfordshire, England	35
8	Henry Krolikowski	Wyandotte, Mich.	30	8	Alexander Kihurani	Mohnton, Pa.	30
9	Dave Hintz	Enumclaw, Wash.	22	8	Rod Hendricksen	Clinton, N.J.	30
9	Ramana Lagemann	Somerville, Mass.	22	10	Mark Williams	N Potomac, Md.	28
11	Amy BeberVanzo	Petaluma, Calif.	20	10	Marc Goldfarb	Atkinson, N.H.	28
12	Patrick Richard	Squamish, B.C. Can.	17	12	Michael Fennell	Kingston	22
12	Tim O'Neil	Dalton, N.H.	17	12	Rick Hintz	El Cajon, Calif.	22
14	Thomas Lawless	Yonkers, N.Y.	16	14	Jeffrey Burmeister	St Louis Park, Minn.	19
14	Otis Dimiters	Great Neck, N.Y.	16	15	Martin Headland	Caledon, Ont. Can.	17
14	George Plsek Jr	Solana Beach, Calif.	16	16	Alan Ockwell	Stouffville, Ont. Can.	16
17	Lauchlin O'Sullivan	San Francisco, Calif.	14	17	Alan Perry	Bainbridge Island, Wash.	14
18	Robert Olson	Eden Prairie, Minn.	13	17	Scott Putnam	Richfield, Minn.	14
19	Antoine L'Estage	St. Jean, Q.C Can.	11	19	Ryan Johnson	Winona, Minn.	13
20	Dennis Martin	Green Bay, Wis.	10	20	John Dillon	Thousand Oaks, Calif.	10
20	Brian Scott	Phoenix, Ariz.	10	21	Pete Gladysz	Troy, Mich.	8
20	Gary Cavett	Kirkland, Wash.	10	21	Brian Sharkey	Aaglenhead, Co Louth	8
23	Michael Hurst	Pendleton, Ind.	8	21	Russell Norton	Fairport, N.Y.	8
23	Doug Shepherd	Plymouth, Mich.	8	24	Faruq Mays	Gaithersburg, Md.	7
25	George Georgakopoulos	Rockville, Md.	7	25	Erik Lee	Belfast, Maine	5
25	Wyeth Gubelmann	Placerville, Colo.	7	25	Duffy Bowers	Afton, Va.	5
27	John Cassidy IV	Bangor, Maine	5	25	Jeff Secor	Hudsonville, Mich.	5
27	Mark McElduff	Chicago, Ill.	5	28	Dennis Hotson	Stillwater, Okla.	3
27	Chris Czyzio	Flushing, Mich.	5	28	Freddy Weil	Montreal, Q.C. Can.	3
27	Charles Kothe	Indianapolis, Ind.	5	28	Jimmy Brandt	Lake Odessa, Mich.	3
31	Andy Brown	Phoenix, Ariz.	4	31	Eddie Fries	Yonkers, N.Y.	2
32	Arthur Odero-Jowi	Arlington, Texas	3	31	John Allen	Bainbridge Island, Wash.	2
32	Chris Rhodes	Kingwood, Texas	3	31	Christine Beavis	San Diego, Calif.	2
32	Jean-Louis Weil	Prevost, Q.C. Can.	3	34	Patrick Walsh	Aberystwytli, Corgdigion	1

Rally America Championship
Final Standings

Open Class

Driver					Co-driver		
Position	Name	From	Total Points		Position	Name	From	Total Points

Position	Name	From	Total Points	Position	Name	From	Total Points
32	Kenny Bartram	Stillwater, Okla.	3	34	Ray Felice	Guelph, Ont. Can.	1
36	Tim Paterson	Issaquah, Wash.	2	34	Jeffrey Becker	New York, N.Y.	1
36	Peter Reilly	Brampton, Ont. Can.	2	34	Alexander Korovkine	Framingham, Mass.	1
36	Seamus Burke	Powder Springs, Ga.	2	34	Mike Rossey	Rochester, Mich.	1
39	Jason Waples	Pueblo, Colo.	1	34	Rebecca Greek	Denver, Colo.	1
39	Dmitri Kishkarev	Ocean, N.J.	1	34	Jeremy Wimpey	Blacksburg, Va.	1
39	Paul Choiniere II	Shelburne, Vt.	1	34	David Dooley	Bronx, N.Y.	1
39	Patrick Lilly	Yonkers, N.Y.	1	34	Damien Irwin	Chicago, Ill.	1
39	Daniel O'Brien	Maspeth, N.Y.	1	34	Jason Takkunen	Anoka, Minn.	1
39	David Anton	Mount Laurel, N.J.	1	34	Noel Gallagher	Yonkers, N.Y.	1
39	Eoin McGeough	Memphis, Tenn.	1	34	Phillip Assad	Brampton, Ont. Can.	1
39	Frank Sprongl	Georgetown, Ont. Can.	1	34	Daniel Sprongl	Mississauga, Can.	1

Group N

Position	Name	From	Total Points	Position	Name	From	Total Points
1	David Anton	Mount Laurel, N.J.	95	1	Dominik Jozwiak	Ridgewood, N.Y.	78
2	Jonathan Bottoms	Buffalo, N.Y.	62	2	Carolyn Bosley	Hinesburg, Vt.	62
3	Andrew Pinker	Perth, Aus.	44	3	Robbie Durant	Oxfordshire, England	44
4	Otis Dimiters	Great Neck, N.Y.	23	4	Alan Ockwell	Stouffville, Ont. Can.	23
5	Wyeth Gubelmann	Placerville, Colo.	22	5	Cynthia Krolikowski	Wyandotte, Mich.	22
6	Ralph Kosmides	Newport Beach, Calif.	17	6	John Dillon	Thousand Oaks, Calif.	17
7	Brendan Kelly	Jamison, Penn.	14	6	Rebecca Greek	Denver, Colo.	17
8	Josh Chang	Allen, Texas	11	8	Keith Boyd	Enniskillen, N. Ireland	14
9	Todd Moberly	Pueblo West, Colo.	1	9	Jeff Cruzan	Allen, Texas	11
10	Ray Moberly	Colorado Springs, Colo.	1				

Rally America Championship
Final Standings

PGT

	Driver					Co-driver		
Position	**Name**	**From**	**Total Points**		**Position**	**Name**	**From**	**Total Points**
1	Matthew Johnson	Apex, N.C.	141		1	Kim DeMotte	St Louis, Mo.	146
2	Tanner Foust	Steamboat Springs, Colo.	93		2	Scott Crouch	Boulder, Colo.	81
3	Eric Langbein	Annapolis, Md.	79		3	Jeremy Wimpey	Blacksburg, Va.	79
4	Patrick Moro	Dublin, Ohio	46		4	Jerry Stang	Marquette, Mich.	35
5	Robert Olson	Eden Prairie, Minn.	39		5	Pamela McGarvey	Columbus, Ohio	29
6	Bryan Pepp	Marquette, Mich.	35		6	Ryan Johnson	Winona, Minn.	27
7	Norm LeBlanc	Pemberton, B.C. Can.	24		7	Keith Morison	Calgary, Alb. Can.	24
8	Tom Young	Brighton, Mich.	22		8	Jim LeBeau	Southfield, Mich.	22
8	Jamie Thomas	Kirkland, Wash.	22		9	Lise Mendham	Lyndeborough, N.H.	18
10	Edward Mendham	Lyndeborough, N.H.	18		10	Carl Fisher	Pittsboro, N.C.	17
11	Greg Drozd	Lyons, Ill.	14		10	Mike Rossey	Rochester, Mich.	17
12	Travis Hanson	Williamsburg, Mich.	12		12	John Nordlie	Bloomington, Minn.	14
13	Wojciech Okula	Bethel, Conn.	6		13	Terry Hanson	Williamsburg, Mich.	12
14	Timothy Penasack	Nashua, N.H.	2		13	Christine Beavis	San Diego, Calif.	12
15	Kazimierz Pudelek	Chicago, Ill.	1		13	Jason Takkunen	Anoka, Minn.	12
15	Timothy Stevens	Wells, Maine	1		16	Adam Pelc	Middle Village, N.Y.	6
15	Nathan Conley	Monument, Colo.	1		17	Chris Stark	Baltimore, Md.	1
15	Joan Hoskinson	Thunder Bay, Ont. Can.	1		17	Brandye Monks	Colorado Springs, Colo.	1
17	Jeff Secor	Hudsonville, Mich.	1					
17	Marc Goldfarb	Atkinson, N.H.	1					
17	Nathalie Richard	Halifax, N.S. Can.	1					
17	Mariusz Malik	Chicago, Ill.	1					

Group 5

	Driver					Co-driver		
1	Bruce Davis	Granite Bay, Calif.	98		1	Jimmy Brandt	Lake Odessa, Mich.	98
2	Cary Kendall	Forest Lake, Minn.	59		2	Scott Friberg	Forest Lake, Minn.	59
3	Jon Hamilton	Marysville, Ohio	41		3	Ken Sabo	Marietta, Ga.	41
4	Eric Burmeister	Dearborn Hts, Mich.	37		4	Dave Shindle	Falls Church, Va.	37
5	Paul Dunn	Oakley, Ill.	34		5	Bill Westrick	Royal Oak, Mich.	34
6	Marcin Kowalski	Darien, Ill.	23		6	Maciej Sawicki	Bartlett, Ill.	23
7	John Conley	Monument, Colo.	22		7	Pete Gladysz	Troy, Mich.	22
7	Doug Shepherd	Plymouth, Mich.	22		7	Steven Treml	Colorado Springs, Colo.	22
9	Andrew Havas	Hopewell Junction, N.Y.	17		9	John Dillon	Thousand Oaks, Calif.	17
10	Andrew Sutherland	Studio City, Calif.	1		10	Christine Beavis	San Diego, Calif.	1

Rally America Championship

Final Standings

Group 2

Driver				Co-driver			
Position	**Name**	**From**	**Total Points**	**Position**	**Name**	**From**	**Total Points**
1	Eric Duncan	Soda Springs, Idaho	64	1	Matt Duncan	Clarkston, Mich.	64
2	Sans Thompson	Grass Valley, Calif.	47	2	Craig Marr	Chico, Calif.	24
3	Daniel Cook	Hinesburg, Vt.	22	3	William Rhodes	Haverford, Pa.	22
3	Chip Miller	Snohomish, Wash.	22	3	Carl Schenk	Ste Anne-de-Bellevue, QC CAN	22
3	Jon Nichols	Pointe-Claire, Q.C. Can.	22	3	David Stone	Acme, Mich.	22
3	James Robinson	Delaware, Ohio	22	3	Andrew Jessup	Raymond, Ohio	22
7	Robin Jones	Vergennes, Vt.	19	3	Kathryn Hansen	Friday Harbor, Wash.	22
8	Christopher Duplessis	Mason Twp, Maine	18	8	William Sekella	Reading, Pa.	19
9	Matt Christensen	Boise, Idaho	17	9	Edward McNelly	Oxford, Maine	18
10	Kenny Bartram	Stillwater, Okla	14	10	Eric Christensen	Boise, Idaho	17
10	Lars Wolfe	Danville, Calif.	14	11	Dennis Hotson	Stillwater, Okla.	14
10	Dan Brosnan	Norwood, Mass.	14	11	Jeffrey Hagan	Whitby, Ont. Can.	14
13	Robert Olson	Eden Prairie, Minn.	1	11	Scot Langford	Springfield, Ore.	14
14	Ryan Johnson	Winona, Minn.	1				

Production

Driver				Co-driver			
1	Kenny Bartram	Stillwater, Okla.	110	1	Dennis Hotson	Stillwater, Okla.	110
2	Kathy Jarvis	Park City, Utah	61	2	Martin Headland	Caledon, Ont. Can.	44
3	Michael Merbach	Appleton, Wis.	40	3	Jeff Feldt	Kaukauna, Wis.	40
4	Jim Stevens	Kingsville, Ont. Can.	31	4	Marianne Stevens	Windsor, Ont. Can.	31
5	Eric Heitkamp	Columbus, Ohio	17	5	Nick Lehner	Dublin, Ohio	17
5	Emily Burton-Weinman	Minneapolis, Minn.	17				
7	Craig Marr	Chico, Calif.	1				

Seamus Burke and Chrissie Beavis (shown at Prescott) win the United States Rally driver and co-driver championships.

United States Rally Championship

Final Championship Standings

Overall 4-Wheel Drive

Driver			Co-driver		
Position	**Name**	**Total Points**	**Position**	**Name**	**Total Points**
1	Seamus Burke	125	1	Christine Beavis	125
2	Wolfgang Hoeck	122	2	Piers O'Hanlon	122
3	Brian Scott	82	3	John Dillon	86
4	George Georgakopoulos	82	4	Faruq Mays	82
5	Wyeth Gubelmann	67	5	Cindy Krolikowski	67
6	George Plsek	58	6	Jeff Burmeister	58
7	Brian Street	54	7	Alan Ockwell	49
8	Gerard Coffey	40	8	Rod Amato	43
9	Randy Dowell	38	9	David Dooley	40
10	Tom Lawless	36	10	Jonathan Schiller	38
10	Travis Pastrana	36	11	Graham Quinn	36
10	Todd Moberly	36	11	Jakke Honkanen	36
11	Ken Block	31	11	Raymond Moberly	36
11	Ralph Kosmides	31	12	Alex Gelsomino	31
12	Blake Yoon	30	13	Robbie Durant	27
13	David Anton	27	13	Jeff Secor	27
13	Gary Cavett	27	14	Nathalie Richard	26
14	Matt Iorio	24	15	Jeremy Wimpey	24
14	Leon Styles	24	15	Mark McAllister	24
15	Daniel O'Brien	22	16	Stephan Duffy	22
15	Craig Studnicky	22	17	Jeffrey Hagan	22
16	Dennis Chizma	20	18	Andrew Cushman	20
16	Nathan Conley	20	18	Brandye Monks	20
17	Otis Dimiters	18	19	Mustafa Samli	17
18	Cem Akdeniz	17	20	David Weiman	15
19	Charlie Donnelly	8	21	Alexander Kihurani	12
19	Amy BeberVanzo	8	22	Bill Westrick	8
19	Mike Whitman	8	23	Barry McCann	4
19	Patrick Farrell	4	23	Bernard Farrell	4
19	Hampton Bridwell	4	23	Joshua Katinger	4
19	Chad Dykes	4	23	Brian Coats	4
19	Gabe vonAhlefeld	4	23	Rick Hintz	4
19	Lauchlin O'Sullivan	4	23	Jody Olson	4
19	Brad Morris	4	23	Ryan Gutile	4
19	Dave Hintz	4			

United States Rally Championship
Final Championship Standings

Driver				Co-driver	

Overall 2-Wheel Drive

Position	Name	Total Points	Position	Name	Total Points
1	Bruce Davis	162	1	Jimmy Brandt	162
2	Kristopher Marciniak	114	2	Christine Wittish	114
3	Jimmey Keeney	67	3	Melissa Salas	36
4	Mark Lawrence	36	4	Robert Maciejski	36
5	Eric Burmeister	31	5	Dave Shindle	31
5	Larry Gross	31	5	Brian Moody	31
6	Michael Taylor	24	5	Doug Young	31
7	Lars Wolfe	22	6	Steve Taylor	24
8	Jeff Rados	18	7	Scott Langford	22
9	Tony Chavez	4	9	Guido Hamacher	18
9	Dave Carapetyan	4	10	Robin Lockhart	4
9	Andrew Lockhart	4	10	Ed Dahl	4
9	Kris Dahl	4	10	Justin Kwak	4
			10	Doug Robinson	4

Open 4-Wheel Drive

Position	Name	Total Points	Position	Name	Total Points
1	Seamus Burke	127	1	Christine Beavis	127
2	Wolfgang Hoeck	127	2	Piers O'Hanlon	127
3	George Georgakopoulas	92	3	Faruq Mays	92
4	Brian Scott	84	4	John Dillon	84
5	George Plsek	62	5	Jeff Burmeister	62
6	Gerard Coffey	42	6	David Dooley	42
6	Randy Dowell	42	6	Jonathan Schiller	42
7	Travis Pastrana	36	7	Graham Quinn	36
7	Tom Lawless	36	7	Jakke Honkanen	36
7	Wyeth Gubelmann	36	7	Cindy Krolikowski	36
7	Todd Moberly	36	7	Raymond Moberly	36
8	Ken Block	31	8	Alex Gelsomino	31
8	Ralph Kosmides	31	8	Alan Ockwell	31
9	Matt Iorio	27	9	Jeremy Wimpey	27
9	Gary Cavett	27	9	Jeff Secor	27
10	Leon Styles	24	10	Nathalie Richard	26
10	Daniel O'Brien	24	11	Stephan Duffy	24
11	Blake Yoon	12	11	Mark McAllister	24

United States Rally Championship
Final Championship Standings

Driver | Co-driver

<u>**Open 4-Wheel Drive**</u>

Position	Name	Total Points		Position	Name	Total Points
12	Charlie Donnelly	8		12	Alexander Kihurani	12
12	Amy BeberVanzo	8		13	Bill Westrick	8
13	Patrick Farrell	4		14	Jeffrey Hagan	4
13	Hampton Bridwell	4		14	Barry McCann	4
13	Craig Studnicky	4		14	Bernard Farrell	4
13	Chad Dykes	4		14	Joshua Katinger	4
13	Gabe vonAhlefeld	4		14	Jody Olson	4
13	Mike Whitman	4		14	Rick Hintz	4
13	Dave Hintz	4		14	Noel Gallagher	4
14	Jeff Burmeister	4				
14	Brian Coats	4				

<u>**Open 2-Wheel Drive**</u>

Position	Name	Total Points		Position	Name	Total Points
1	Bruce Davis	162		1	Jimmy Brandt	162
2	Jimmey Keeney	63		2	Melissa Salas	36
3	Mark Lawrence	36		3	Robert Maciejski	36
4	Eric Burmeister	31		4	Dave Shindle	31
4	Larry Gross	31		4	Brian Moody	31
5	Lars Wolfe	24		4	Doug Young	31
6	Jeff Rados	22		5	Scott Langford	24
7	Dave Carapetyan	4		6	Guido Hamacher	22
7	Andrew Lockhart	4		7	Ryan Gutile	4
7	Brad Morris	4		7	Robin Lockhart	4
7	Tony Chavez	4		7	Justin Kwak	4
				7	Doug Robinson	4

<u>**Superstock**</u>

Position	Name	Total Points		Position	Name	Total Points
1	Brian Street	36		1	Andrew Cushman	36
1	Dennis Chizma	36		1	Brandye Monks	36
1	Nathan Conley	36		2	David Weinmam	36
2	Lauchlin O'Sullivan	4			John Dillon	4

United States Rally Championship
Final Championship Standings

Driver				Co-driver		

Group N

Position	Name	Total Points		Position	Name	Total Points
1	Brian Street	63		1	Rob Amato	63
2	Wyeth Gubelmann	36		2	Cindy Krolikowski	36
3	David Anton	36		3	Robbie Durant	36
	Cem Akdeniz	36			Mustafa Samli	36
	Craig Studnicky	31			Jeff Hagan	31
	Otis Dimiters	31			Alan Ockwell	18

Stock

Position	Name	Total Points		Position	Name	Total Points
1	Kristopher Marciniak	139		1	Christine Wittish	139
2	Michael Taylor	36		2	Steven Taylor	36
3	Kris Dahl	4		3	Ed Dahl	4

Organization Contacts

	Location	**Web Address**
Rally America Championship		www.rally-america.com
Sno*Drift Rally	Atlanta, Michigan	www.sno-drift.org
Rally in the 100 Acre Wood	Salem, Missouri	www.100aw.org
Oregon Trail Rally	Hillsboro, Oregon	www.oregontrailrally.com
Susquehannock Trail Performance Rally (STPR)	Wellsboro, Pennsylvania	www.stpr.org
Maine Forest Rally	Newry, Maine	www.maineforestrally.com
Ojibwe Forests Rally	Bemidji, Minnesota	www.ojibweforestrally.com
Colorado Cog Rally	Steamboat Springs, Colorado	www.coloradocogrally.com
Lake Superior Performance Rally (LSPR)	Houghton, Michigan	www.lsprorally.com
Wild West Rally	Olympia, Washington	www.wildwestrally.org
United States Rally Championship		www.unitedstatesrallychampionship.com
Rally New York	Monticello, New York	www.rallynewyork.com
Subaru Rim of the World Rally	Lancaster, California	www.rimoftheworldrally.com
Olympus International Rally	Olympia, Washington	www.olympusrally.com
Rally Tennessee	Linden, Tennessee	www.rallytennessee.com
Prescott Rally	Prescott, Arizona	www.prescottrally.com
Laughlin International Rally	Laughlin, Nevada	www.rallyusa.com
Other Contacts		
World Rally Championship		www.wrc.com
Corona Rally México	León, México	www.rallymexico.com

SPEED-PICS

To purchase additional copies of this book or copies of Volume 1, please contact your original supplier or write to:

SPEED-PICS Publishing
6101 Long Prairie Road #744-110
Flower Mound, TX 75028
www.speed-pics.com

About the Author

After gaining a degree from Queen's University, Belfast (United Kingdom), Ronnie Arnold spent more than twenty-five years in the technology industry. His experience ranges from ten years as a consultant based in Belfast and London to being chief technology officer for a startup in Silicon Valley, California.

Recently he changed career to focus on his long-term passion of photography, specializing in motor sport—rallies and road races.

His interest in motor sport started in Northern Ireland where he competed as a driver and co-driver in regional rally and sprint events—gaining his International Rally Driver's License in the early 1970s.

He was a member of council and press officer for the Ulster Automobile Club (best known for the Circuit of Ireland International Rally). He edited the club's *Wheelspin* magazine, was a member of the competitions committee and was heavily involved in the organization of the circuit. His images have been published in magazines, newspapers and on Web sites.

Arnold lives in Highland Village, Texas. He is a member of the Professional Photographers of America.